Olive Oil

Nutrition
and good health

ATHENS

Summer Dream® EDITIONS

32 Aeropis Str. 118 52 Athens
Tel.: (210) 34.50.471 Fax: (210) 34.59.114

Summer Dream® EDITIONS

Publisher: S. & I. Kontaratos Co.
Editing: Si Enorasis Advertising
Translation: Avraam Loucaides – A-Z Services
Photographs: Studio Koutoulias
N. Arampatzis
Food Stylist: Maria Sandilou
Recipe Text: Maria Sandilou
Printing: HAIDEMENOS S.A.
Binding: Iliopoulos – Rodopoulos

ISBN 960-7439-41-4

CONTENTS
periehomena

APPETISERS

PIES

SALADS

PASTA & RICE

MEALS IN OIL & LENTEN FOOD

FISH & SEAFOOD

MEAT & POULTRY

SWEETS

INTRODUCTION
esagogi

HISTORY

*"The goddess Athena cast her eyes on the beautiful city.
That's where she wanted to go and stay so as to protect it.
But someone else had set his eye on the same city: The god of the sea, Poseidon!*

-- Very well, said the goddess, who was always just.
*-- Let us contest each other, each offering the best of whatever he/she has in this city,
and whoever wins, the city will be theirs.*

*They elected Cecrops to be judge. Cecrops was half snake,
but was very intelligent, even though he was half man.*

*In the beautiful city that they both loved, there was a rock.
The rock of the Acropolis. They climbed to the top for their contentions.*

*Poseidon struck the rock with his trident and immediately water sprouted out.
Everyone was amazed. What greater gift for a city than that of running water!
Cecrops bowed to taste the water, but it was seawater.*

*Athena knelt and planted a tree.
This was the first olive tree. Athena was declared the winner.
And since then the city was named Athena or Athens.
Olive trees filled the city, as well as throughout Greece.*

Today, every house, every kitchen has the oil and the olives of the tree."
From the book by Sofia Zarabouka, "Mythology for Children".

This is the myth as to how the olive tree was born, a gift to man from the gods, a sacred tree, a majestic commodity. A tree that gives sweet, oily seeds that may easily be preserved for a long period of time, offering strength and health. Their golden-yellow juice -olive oil- gives tastiness and flavour to food, and gives it that extra nutrition. Man learnt to cook with olive oil, to lighten up the dark nights by burning its oil in lanterns, to clean up his wounds and to heal himself of sickness, to beautify his body and to produce culture.

A tree with strong wood. Hercules himself used this wood to fashion his club, which he used in his labours. According to mythology, Hercules in his Cretan form as Ideos Hercules, invited his brothers to a race, where for the first time the winner was crowned by a wreath made from the branch of the wild olive tree that he himself had planted in Olympia. Since then, all the winners at the Olympic Games were awarded a similar wreath made from the branches of the olive tree, as a symbol of peace and conciliation between the races. This wreath is the epitome of the spirit of the Olympic Games, which is that of noble competition. It was considered to be the greatest honour and Olympic winners basked in glory. The olive wreath was even considered to be above life itself, which is verified by the inscription on a plain headstone dating back to the 3rd Century A.D., which stated that the deceased, in his dying breath during a wresting match prayed to Zeus, "a wreath or death".

A tree that grows both in fertile plains as well as on tough slopes, and even next to the sea. All it needs to develop is sun and the pleasant, temperate Mediterranean climate.

A tree whose existence dates back thousands of years, back to the beginning of history. The petrified leaves of the wild olive tree -dated 50,000 - 60,000 years- that were discovered in Caldera on Santorini confirm its antiquity, while also linking mythology to reality. In Zakro on Crete, a conic ceramic cup full of olives was discovered inside a well. Its age: 3,500 years! Fortunately the archaeologists were able to photograph these "fresh" olives before they decomposed, as soon as they came into contact with the air and the sun.

Archaeological findings in Knossos and Faistos, dating back 3,000 years, included earthenware jars used to store olive oil, fresco depictions, jewellery and coins which indicated that the then inhabitants were aware of the value of olive oil.

The systematic cultivation of the olive tree by the Minoan civilisation opened the way for it to spread throughout the Mediterranean region, The ideograms discovered in Knossos, Pilo and Mycenae are written proof of this fact.

In the 8th Century BC, the olive tree was known throughout the islands in the Aegean, as witnessed by Homer in his Iliad and Odysseus, which contain references to the olive tree and to olive oil. He describes with awe "the rich gifts given to Alcinous (King of Phaeacia) by the gods", that included "fresh olives from the garden which the slaves "grounded the seed which was as gold as an apple".

Since the olive tree was a sacred tree, it was forbidden to cut or to burn it, as decreed by special laws enacted by the Athenian Republic in the 5th Century BC, and the penalty was ostracism or even confiscation of the culprit's property. As it was considered to be a tree of great value, an olive wreath was hung outside the door of the house when a boy was born. During the Panathenian festival when athletic games took place, the prize was the Panathenian oil, - that is, the oil from the sacred olives of Athena - which was given to the winners in painted earthenware vessels.

OLIVE OIL & RELIGION

Olive oil is indissolubly linked to the religious and devotional traditions of the Orthodox Church. It is a significant aspect dominant in the confirmation rites for priests, Holy Unction and baptisms. During the baptismal rites the priest pours a little olive oil into the font. He makes the sign of the cross on the body and head of the baby that he is baptising with the three fingers that he has rinsed with the olive oil. The godparent then anoints the baby's body with oil. After the baptismal service has finished, the water with the oil remains in the font. It is considered sacred and should never be poured down a drain or thrown away. In olden times the water was poured into the sea, but today it is emptied into special tanks buried next to the church. The baptismal clothes that have been soaked with olive oil, are also washed in the sea, or the water in which they have been washed is poured into the sea or river or lake.

Olive oil burns in the small oil-lamp vigils in churches, as well as in oil-lamps in homes next to the icons. The oil from the oil-lamps is considered to have therapeutic and sedative properties. It is rubbed into the areas of the body that are painful, as well as on the forehead of those suffering from spiritual illnesses. In raging storms, sailors poured some oil into the sea and at the same time lowered the icon of Saint Nicolas, in order to appease the sea and turn it into a "sea of oil".

Finally, oil is added to the holy dough of bread and the consecrated bread offered by the faithful to the church so that they may be blessed by the priest. Olive oil is also one of the nine ingredients used to make the "Fanouropita" on August 27th, the festival of Saint Fanourios. Olive oil is also a main ingredient in many island dishes that are cooked during the fasting periods of Lent, Easter, Christmas and August 15th.

THERAPEUTIC & BEAUTIFYING PROPERTIES

The therapeutic properties of olive oil have been known since ancient times. Various usages are described in texts by Hippocrates. Common practice was to either anoint the body and place poultices on the wounds or to give preparations to the patients to drink.

Even today olive oil is considered to be a purgative antidote in cases of poisoning and a balsam anointment to soothe pain and heal wounds.

In many parts of Greece, bandages soaked in olive oil are used for sprains. Anointment with olive oil also soothes the body in cases of burns, insect bites and skin disorders. A spoonful of oil every morning is thought to heal stomach and bile disorders, and many people believe that it is the perfect pick-me-up after too much drinking!

Oil even helps in the removal of plant and urchin thorns from plants and urchins. In ancient times the body was anointed with olive oil for purposes of cleanliness and hygiene. Women anointed their bodies with oil to beautify themselves and rubbed scented oil into their hair. Even today rubbing oil in scalp hair is thought to prevent alopecia, as it gives health and beauty to hair, as well as to the facial skin and nails.

Green or white soap made from olive oil is also considered to be a pure cosmetic for the face, body and hair. Even detergent companies are now offering this soap in powder form for the washing of baby clothes because it does not cause skin disorders and eczemas.

According to popular perception, another property of olive oil is its aphrodisiac capabilities. It is thought to give lovers more erotic power and stamina, giving rise to the saying: "Eat oil and come at night", which is a well-known adage throughout Greece. However, this perception may not be a Greek invention, since the Spanish writer Manuel Velasqueth Montalbran mentions in his Immoral Recipes: "Oil is an oleaginous substance that accompanies a kiss".

OLIVE OIL & HEALTH

From the age of Hippocrates to today many studies have shown the nutritional value of olive oil and its contribution to our health. The consumption of olive oil supplies us with large quantities of monounsaturated lipid or fatty acids, since they comprise approximately 73.7% of olive oil.

In order for us to understand why this is significant for our health, we should consider the following: The different kinds of lipid or fatty substances found in foodstuffs contain two kinds of fatty acids in proportions that fluctuate for each kind: saturated and unsaturated.

Saturated fatty acids are found in large concentrations in animal foodstuffs, such as meat and its fat, milk, butter and dairy products.

Unsaturated fatty acids are found in large concentrations in oils derived from plants and fish. Unsaturated fatty acids are divided into polyunsaturated and monounsaturated.

OLIVE OIL CONTENTS PER 100 gr.	
MONOUNSATURATED FATTY ACIDS	73,7 gr
SATURATED FATTY ACIDS	13,5 gr
POLYUNSATURATED FATTY ACIDS	8,4 gr
CHOLESTEROL	0 mg
VITAMIN E	12.400 mg
ENERGY	884 kcal

USDA Nutrient Database for Standard Reference, Release 14 (July 2001)

Polyunsaturated fatty acids: Found in large concentrations in various seed oils, such as sunflower oil, soya-bean oil, cottonseed oil, maize oil.

Monounsaturated fatty acids: Found in large concentrations in olive oil.

Recent research work has shown that saturated fatty acids increase LDL levels -i.e. the so-called "bad" cholesterol- in the blood, which is responsible for clogging of arteries, due to the fatty deposits on their inner walls, resulting in arteriosclerosis.

In contrast, a diet that includes foodstuffs containing mainly monounsaturated fatty acids is beneficial because not only does it not increase LDL levels, it reduces these levels and at the same time increases HDL levels, i.e. that of "good" cholesterol. It is thought that HDL prevents LDL deposits on the walls of the arteries,. It rather propels LDL it to the liver for renewed processing or to the excretory system.

As with monounsaturated fatty acids, polyunsaturated fatty acids do not burden the body with LDL, but according to recent studies they have the disadvantage of reducing HDL levels to a certain degree.

FATTY SUBSTANCE CONTENTS PER 100 gr.			
Type of Fatty Substance	Monounsaturates %	Polyunsaturates %	Saturates %
Olive Oil	74	8	14
Maize oil	24	59	13
Soya-bean oil	23	59	14
Sunflower oil	20	66	10
Cottonseed oil	18	52	26

The Wellness Encyclopedia

Olive Oil and the Heart:

Research on nutrition has shown that the total amount as well as the type of fatty substances that we intake plays a significant role in the health of the cardiovascular system, as well as their saturated, monounsaturated and polyunsaturated proportions. The consumption of olive oil ensures the necessary intake of monounsaturates that -as was stated previously- act positively in increasing HDL levels and decreasing LDL levels. Thus, this type of sustenance diet can contribute to the healthy functions of the cardiovascular system, control hypertension and reduce the risk of cardiac disorders such as coronary disease and heart attack.

Researchers' interest in the contributions of nutrition -and especially that of fatty substances- for a healthy body was rekindled by the results from the Seven Country Study by Dr. Ancel Benjamin Keys in 1950, who studied the nutritional habits of a sample of the male population from seven countries: America, Finland, Holland, Italy, Yugoslavia, Japan and Greece. The study showed that for Crete -where olive oil consumption is high- the number of cardiac diseases in 13,000 men aged between 40 and 59 and over a 15 year period, was the lowest of the seven countries. In comparison to the population samples from the other countries, it was:

- 55 times lower than the Finnish
- 37 times lower than the Americans
- 21 times lower than the Italians
- 8 times lower than the Japanese

After a series of similar research programs, it is now known that the monounsaturated fatty acids found in olive oil contribute positively to the prevention of cardiac diseases, in contrast to saturated, which act negatively.

Olive Oil and Cancer:

Many scientists, and especially the research performed by Sir Richard Doll, English epidemiologist and Nobelist, have shown that there is a relation between the high consumption of foodstuffs containing fatty substances -even in the form of polyunsaturatesd- and some forms of cancer. At the same time, scientists have turned their attention to the antioxidant substances found in olive oil, such as Vitamin E, one of the basic antioxidants that protect cells from oxidation and deterioration, which may lead to carcinogenesis.

Olive Oil, Obesity and Diabetes:

Correct nutrition and weight reduction are critical factors in combating diabetes. The systematic consumption of olive oil helps to reduce lipid levels and regulate sugar in the blood. It also remains longer in the stomach than saturated lipids and thus the feeling of hunger in persons trying to lose weight is not generated shortly after a meal in persons trying to lose weight.

Olive Oil and the Peptic Digestive System:

Existing research has shown that there is a direct link between the consumption of olive oil and the natural functions of the peptic digestive system. It helps in balancing gastric acid secretions, prevents cholelithiasis and in general, contributes positively to metabolic functions through the peptic digestive system.

MEDITERRANEAN DIET

In 1948 researchers from the Rockefeller Institute studied - after an invitation from the Greek Government - the nutritional habits of the inhabitants of Crete in order to reach a conclusion as to how developed countries may help undeveloped countries through correct nutrition. Taking in account the results of this study, we can safely say to the Greek Government: "Leave the Cretans alone!"

Despite the fact that the Seven Countries Study clearly indicated that the nutritional habits of the Mediterranean countries advocate "good and correct" nutrition, only in the last ten years have a large number of research programs recommending and supporting this Study come to light.

The Mediterranean countries (Southern Europe, North Africa, the Mid-East) all basically follow a common nutritional model which is called the Mediterranean Diet and is based on:

"the consumption of a large quantity of cereals, legumes, vegetables and fruit, a moderate consumption of milk and dairy products, fish and poultry and a small consumption of red meat with the exclusive consumption of olive oil".

These ascertainments and the definition of what constitutes the Mediterranean Diet, as well as its benefits to the human body, were announced at an International Convention for the Nutritional Habits of Mediterranean Countries, which took place in Massachusetts in the United States in January 1993. The findings of this Convention, together with the schematic representation of the Mediterranean Diet in the form of a pyramid, were published in a supplementary issue of the American Journal of Clinical Nutrition.

MEDITERRANEAN DIET PYRAMID

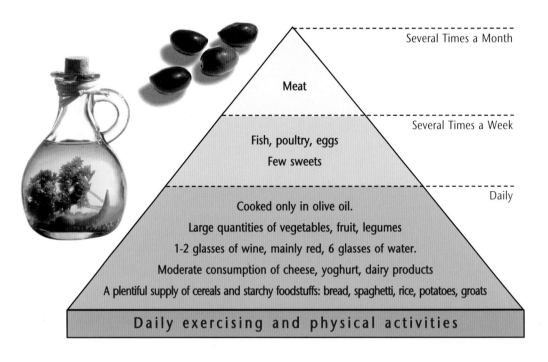

Several Times a Month

Meat

Several Times a Week

Fish, poultry, eggs

Few sweets

Daily

Cooked only in olive oil.

Large quantities of vegetables, fruit, legumes

1-2 glasses of wine, mainly red, 6 glasses of water.

Moderate consumption of cheese, yoghurt, dairy products

A plentiful supply of cereals and starchy foodstuffs: bread, spaghetti, rice, potatoes, groats

Daily exercising and physical activities

OLIVE OIL QUALITY

The quality of olive oil was prescribed by the International Council on Olive Oil and is subject to European Union regulations. Olive oil is mainly characterised by its acidity; i.e. by its acid concentration, which other than quality, also affects its taste as well as its nutritional value. Acidity up to 3.3% is acceptable. Other factors that affect olive oil are its oxidation or "tanginess" that gives an unpleasant flavour, is harmful and therefore unsuitable for consumption. The tanginess of olive oil is the result of its agedness and the unsuitable method of storage; in other words, in a place exposed to light, air and heat or stored in a container that oxidises. For these reasons olive oil should be stored in glass or ceramic containers or in other types of containers that do not oxidise, in a cool and dark place.

The quality of the olive oil also depends on other factors such as the land and climatic conditions where the olive trees grow, the use of chemical pesticides, the natural use of fertilisers, the method of harvesting, the degree of the olive seed's maturity and the various ways of processing the seeds in the olive press in order to extract the olive oil.

Category	Description	Acidity
Exceptionally Virgin Olive Oil	The naturally fruity taste and aroma of a fresh olive, with an oily greenish-yellow colour. When very fresh, it has a density that gives it its cloudy appearance.	< 1.0 %
Virgin Olive Oil	Exceptionally refined taste and aroma of an olive, with an oily or oily-yellow colour.	< 2.0 %
Common Virgin Olive Oil	Rich "oily" taste and aroma, lovely shiny colour.	< 3.3 %
Refined Olive Oil	An olive oil with a large acid concentration (<3.3) which has undergone a refining process. Has no characteristic taste and aroma, with a lucent, light yellow colour.	< 3.3 %
Pure Olive Oil	A mixture of refined olive oil and virgin olive oil. A pleasant taste with a yellow-green colour.	< 1.5 %

Care is needed when buying "anonymous" olive oil; i.e., olive oil that is not approved and has no label describing its quality and ingredients. It is best to avoid this type of oil because it has no quality criteria and on many occasions it is unsuitable or of bad quality. You should always read the label when buying olive oil so as to assure yourself that the product is suitable and is in compliance with all prescribed specifications.

In recent years excellent quality olive oil is also being produced biologically. Biologically cultivated olive oil is subject to special regulations specified by the European Union. This cultivation requires especial handling which begins from the planting of the trees, a ban on the use of chemical fertilisers and insecticides and includes harvesting methods and the methods used to crush the seeds to extract the olive oil. The attributes of biologically produced olive oil must be clearly stated on the label.

TEN POINTS CONCERNING OLIVE OIL

From the Program for the Promotion of Olive Oil Consumption by the European Union

There are ten points about olive oil that we should all know and use on a daily basis. These will help us not only to get acquainted with it, but also to take advantage of all its amazing qualities for a healthy diet, These will help us not only to know more about this healthy nutrition but also to utilise all its amazing properties that are needed by modern man.

1. It may act as a substitute for butter in cooking.
2. It is by nature the best oil for frying.
3. For an even healthier dish, it can be added at the end of cooking.
4. Mixed with various spices (garlic, fresh pepper, estragon, cloves, oregano, basil, mint, etc.), it may be a substitute for pre-cooked sauces in salads, fish or meat.
5. Not only is it not heavy, it is easily digested by the peptic digestive system.
6. It is no more fattening than other oils because it contains the same number of calories.
7. It helps in the correct development of the nervous system.
8. It helps to prevent cardiovascular diseases.
9. Olive oil means both physical and spiritual health together.
10. Olive oil plays a significant role in the formation of a balanced food diet for man.

HOW DO WE COOK WITH OLIVE OIL

Category	Description
Exceptionally Virgin Olive Oil	Ideal for food that does not have to be cooked: on toasted bread or toast, in salads and wild greens, as a sauce with lemon, in various dips such as taramosalata (fish roe), tzatziki (cucumber + yoghurt + garlic), skordalia (garlic) and melitzanosalata (eggplant).
Virgin Olive Oil	Ideal for light foods and may also be added raw after the cooking phase: roasted and boiled meats, fish, eggs, salads with boiled vegetables, legumes, oily foods based on oil, without tomato sauce.
Common Olive Oil	For all dishes, including oven or pot roast , oily foods based on oil with tomato sauce, in pies, sweets and for frying.
Refined Olive Oil	Suitable for sweets, cakes, cookies, skaltsounia (type of sweet), when we do not want the characteristic smell of olive oil. For the same reason it is also suitable for mayonnaise.
Pure Olive Oil	Suitable for all uses without of course having the value, taste and aroma of virgin olive oil.

Olive oil is suitable for all types of cooking, but special note should be made for frying with olive oil, as there still seems to be an erroneous misconception as to its suitability.

In Greece frying is traditionally carried out with olive oil, since the various seed oils were unknown to the Greek housewife. When the latter became more well-known, they were taken to be more lighter and thus more suitable for frying, and they had less calories.

This conception however was probably formulated by sources derived from Northern Europe and America where there was excessive usage of animal fatty substances, which were of course much more healthier when compared to seed oils. This however is of no concern to Greek cuisine, which has little use for animal fats. But as was mentioned previously, olive oil is the most healthiest fatty substance with endless benefits to our health and there is therefore no reason to substitute it with seed oils. In fact, the opposite is true.

Especially for frying purposes, it has been observed that olive oil –due to its large concentration of monounsaturates, even when heated to temperatures exceeding 200°C, does not lose its attributes, nor does it oxidise. In contrast, both animal fats which are rich is saturated fats, as well as seed oils, which contains a large number of polyunsaturates, oxidise in temperatures over 160-170°C and thus produce toxic substances that are harmful to the body.

In addition, foods that have been fried in olive oil do not absorb much oil because a crispy crust is formed externally, while internally they maintain their moisture and their flavour. The secret in how to fry correctly is to have the oil at a high temperature in order to form this crust. The secret for correct frying is high temperature oil, so as to form this crust.

Olive oil also can be reused 5-6 times (some maintain up to 10 times) in contrast to other fatty substances, without losing its health values, because it does not break up easily.

OLIVES

The nutritional value of the olive is probably even greater than that of olive oil because it has not undergone any form of processing and thus maintains all its properties to the fullest. Olives are divided into edible olives, which are suitable for eating purposes, and oil- extracting olives, which are used chiefly for the extraction of olive oil. There are however certain mixed varieties that are suitable for eating as well as for producing olive oil.

Olives cannot be eaten directly from the tree because they are bitter. They have to undergo a certain procedure that is described below. The only exception is the "throumbes" or raisin-like olives (also called "roupades" in Lesvbos), which fall off the tree when they ripen and shrivel up ("wrinkled"). These olives are sweet and must be eaten within a few days because salt or other preservatives are not added. However, they can be maintained in excellent condition in the freezer.

Various well-known types of olives that are on the market include "Kalamon" olives with their pointed ends, the large rounded "Amfissis" olives, the wrinkled olives from Thasos, the "Psilolies", olives that are very small olives from Crete and Mani, the "Megaritikes", etc.

Olives may be coloured The colour of olives, which may be green, purple, dark purple, dark brown and black, is not due to a special variety, but rather to their degree of ripening.

TYPES OF OLIVES

EDIBLE VARIETIES FOR THE TABLE

NAME	DESCRIPTION	CULTIVATION AREA
Kalamon Other names: Kalamatiani, Aetonychi, Chondrolia, Korakolia	Medium-sized, walnut almond shaped, curved more on the one side, with a pointed end. Is consumed when very ripe, when the fruit is black.	Peloponnese, Crete, Western Greece
Konservolia Other names: Amfissas, Agriniou, Artas, Voliotiki, Chontrolia, Strongylolia	Large-sized, spherical shaped, oval-like. Is consumed when green, light coloured or black.	Epirus, Roumeli, Boeotia, Thessaly, Euboea, Sporades.
Karydolia Other names: Stravolia, Karolia, Kourolia	Very large-sized, as depicted by the name. Long oval-shaped. Eaten when green, light coloured or black.	Ionian Islands, Chalkidiki, Lesvbos, Euboea, Roumeli
Kolymbades Other names: Kolymbati, Milolia,, Stroumboulolia	Medium-sized, spherical shaped. Eaten very ripe, when the fruit is black.	Fokida, Attica, Cyclades, Messinia
Adrokarpi Other names: Koromilolia, Gaidourolia, Damaskinati, Ispaniki	Quite large. Shaped like a date. Eaten when green.	

VARIETIES THAT PRODUCE OLIVE OIL

NAME	DESCRIPTION	CULTIVATION AREA
Koroneiki Other names: Psilolia, Ladolia, Lianolia	Small-sized, spherical and oval shaped. Gives 15-27 kg. (33 – 59.4 lb.) olive oil per 100 kg. (220 lb.) olives	Peloponnese, Crete, Cyclades, Ionian Islands
Koutsourelia Other names: Patrini, Patrini ladolia	Small-sized, spherical and oval shaped. Gives 20-24 kg. (44 – 52.8 lb.) olive oil per 100 kg. (220 lb.) olives	Peloponnese, Mainland Greece

Types of Olives

Tsounati Other names: Tsounolia, Matsolia, Mouratolia	Small-sized, oval-shaped with a characteristic nipple-shaped end. Gives 25-28 kg. 55 – 61.6 lb.) olive oil per 100 kg. (220 lb.) olives	Peloponnese, Crete
Lianolia Kerkiras (Corfu) Other names: Dafnofylli, Nerolia, Korfolia, Prevezana	Small-sized, oval-shaped. Gives very good quality olive oil, approximately 20 kg. (44 lb.) olive oil per 100 kg. (220 lb.) olives	Ionian Islands, Epirus coast

MIXED VARIETIES

NAME	DESCRIPTION	CULTIVATION AREA
Adramytini Other names: Aivaliotiki, Kasdaglitissa, Frangolia	Medium-sized, spherical and oval shaped. Gives good quality olive oil, 20-23 kg. (44–50.6 lb.) olive oil per 100 kg. (220 lb.) olives, as well as being edible.	Lesvbos, Chios, Andros, Euboea
Valanolia Other names: Kolovi, Mytilinia	Medium-sized, acorn shaped. Gives 25-28 kg. (55–61.6 lb.) of exceptional olive oil per 100kg. (220 lb.) olives, as well as being edible.	Lesvbos, Chios
Throumbolia Other names: Throumba, Thasou, Ladolia, Chondrolia, Stafidolia, Poupada	Medium-sized, oval-shaped. Gives over 25 kg. (55lb.) "sweet-tasting" olive oil per 100 kg. (220 lb.) olives, as well as edible throumbes for the table.	Crete, Attica, Boeotia, Thasos, Cyclades, Northern Aegean Island
Manaki Other names: Kothreiki, Manakolia, Korinthiaki, Glykomanaki	Medium-sized, spherically-shaped. Give exceptionally good quality olive oil, approximately 20 kg. (44 lb.) per 100 kg. (220 lb.) olives, as well as very tasty, edible olives.	Delphi, Amfissa, Kynouria, Ermioni, Poros
Megaritiki Other names: Perachoritiki, Chondrolia, Ladolia	Large-sized, spherically-shaped. Give good quality olive oil, 15-25 kg. (33 – 55 lb.) per 100 kg. (220 lb.) olives, as well as edible olives that can also be consumed green	Mainland Greece, Attica, Boeotia

THE SECRETS OF THE OLIVE

Making the olives less bitter

1. We score the flesh of the olive lengthwise, one or two times, depending on the size of the olive, (several two transverse cuts) without reaching the pit., in proportion to the size of the olive. Small olives do not have to be scored. You can make the incision with a sharp, pointed knife -a cutter or razor blade would be better- so as not to damage the flesh of the olive.

2. We immerse the scored grooved olives into a water-filled container and cover them for 10-15 days, changing the water daily. We taste them every day and when they have sweetened to the degree that we want, we place them in brine.

3. To prepare the brine, we boil coarse sea salt with water until the salt dissolves. The ratio is approximately 1 part salt to 10 parts water. Then we place an egg into the brine to check it. If the egg remains at the bottom of the container, the brine needs more salt. We add just enough salt so that the egg rises to the surface of the brine and floats a little outside the water (thus forming a diameter of about 2-3 cm).

Preserving the olives

1. Olives can be preserved inside brine for long periods of time. When we want to eat them, we wash them very well in running water or leave them for a few hours in a bowl full of water to "de-salt" them. Olives are always stored in glass or ceramic containers.

2. Once we have completed the procedure where we "sweetened" the olives by making them less bitter, we leave them for several days in brine, then for a few more days in water mixed with vinegar (ratio of 1:3). Finally, we remove them from the vinegar and place them in olive oil in a vase.

3. Another method for preserving olives is to place them –after the "sweetening" process- in brine mixed with vinegar (ratio of 3:1), then adding a little olive oil. They can also be stored in a jar with olive oil mixed with a little vinegar.

4. Dry aromatic herbs can be added to the olives in the jars, including oregano, coriander, thyme, bay leaves, hot peppers, garlic, slices of lemon, orange, bitter orange, etc.

5. Olives can be preserved in coarse salt instead of brine. You first place the olives in a basket so as not to collect the liquid emerging from the olives, due to the salt. The ratio is about 150-200 gr. coarse sea salt for every kilogram of olives. When the olives have wrinkled and acquired their flavour, they are ready to be eaten.

6. The preservation procedure for green olives should be carried out early in Autumn when they are still unripe, before they turn black. They are traditionally gathered after the festival of the Cross (14th September). These olives are not scored, they are crushed with a hammer or a stone, pulverising the flesh while trying not to break the pit. This is followeding by the "sweetening" process. Once the bitterness has been removed from the olives, they are stored in coarse salt, (described above). Green olives must be eaten within a short period of time, because after a while they blacken and spoil. You can, of course keep them in the freezer.

THE SHORT DICTIONARY
OF COOKING TERMS

Warming: Used mainly for vegetables. We place the vegetables (or other ingredients mentioned in the recipes) in boiling water, leave for 2' - 3' and then strain immediately.

Boiling: Put all the ingredients mentioned in the recipes in boiling water and leave to macerate as long as necessary to become tender, while the water is boiling continuously.

Simmering: Cooking food in a littler water or sauce that is cooking on a low fire. Simmering is carried out by keeping the pot covered so as not to allow the liquid to evaporate and the food to scorch at the bottom of the pot.

Setting: Thickening of the sauce, which is carried out when all the liquid is absorbed and only the fatty ingredients it contains remains. We can also thicken the sauce by adding eggs, corn- flour, flour or milk cream.

Sautéing: On a high fire, continuously stir the pieces of the ingredients referred to in the recipe with a little olive oil or other fatty substance, until they brown and acquire a golden brown colour.

Frying: Cooking in a frying pan or frying pot with plenty of hot olive oil, or other fatty substance, until the food acquires a dark golden colour.

Roasting: Cooking in the oven, in a roaster or on coals (barbecuing) until the food acquires a dark golden colour. Roasted foods should be coated with olive oil or other fatty substance, otherwise they will dry out.

Toasting: This is a procedure where we place the cooked food under the grill for as few minutes to brown; e.g. a food that has been sprinkled with cheese placed under the grill for a few minutes to brown and the cheese to melt.

Dough rest: Some types of dough, once their ingredients have been mixed, must remain covered for the time specified in the recipe, before they are used (e.g. before we open them into pastry sheets). This procedure is necessary because it facilitates that which we are trying to do.

Dough rising: Dough that contains yeast must be left for a certain period of time in a warm place to allow the yeast to act and double in volume before being used.

Sprinkling: A light covering of the food or sweet with various solid ingredients that are in powder or finely cut form, such as salt, pepper, grated toast, oregano, parsley, sugar, etc.

Equivalencies

1 cup	olive oil	220 gr. (7.7 oz.)
1 cup	butter	225 gr. (7.9 oz.)
1 cup	flour	125 gr. (4.4 oz.)
1 cup	sugar	225 gr. (7.9 oz.)
1 cup	icing sugar	150 gr. (5.3 oz.)
1 cup	milk	240 gr. (8.4 oz.)
1 cup	milk cream	225 gr. (7.9 oz.)
1 cup	water	240 gr. (8.4 oz.)
1 cup	rice	225 gr. (7.9 oz.)
1 cup	grated cheese	110 gr. (3.8 oz.)

Explanation of Abbreviations

cup = cupful

s.s. = soupspoon

t.s. = teaspoon

Degree of difficulty:
◐△△ = simple △◐△ = somewhat difficult
△△◐ = relatively difficult

Nutritional value:
◐△△ = low △◐△ = medium △△◐ = high

Taste:
◐△△ = unobtrusive △◐△ = intense △△◐ = spicy

APPETISERS

orektika

GARLIC SAUCE
skordalia

Serves: 4-6

Preparation time: 30'   Cooking time: no cooking required   Degree of difficulty: ❍△△   Nutritional value: △❍△
Taste: △△❍   Calories: 317

Preparation

3 slices dry bread
2 s.s. vinegar or lemon juice
3-4 cloves mashed garlic
½ cup olive oil
salt and pepper

1. Soak the bread in water, and when soft, remove the crust.
Squeeze the bread between your palms to remove most of the water.
2. Put all the ingredients into the glass container of the blender and beat until all the ingredients have been well mixed and has set.

Alternative: Add at the end of the skordalia 2 s.s. walnuts or blanched almond nuts which have been cut into large pieces. If you want the skordalia to be creamier, you can replace the bread with boiled potatoes that has been mashed.

Note: The mixture should not be beaten in the blender for a long period of time because it will curdle. If this happens, you can "set" the mixture again by adding a little lukewarm water in small doses. If the mixture still does not set, carry out the following: Remove the mixture from the bowl of the blender and wash the latter. In the now clean bowl put in 1 egg yolk and slowly pour in the garlic mixture until it becomes uniform again.

FISH ROE SALAD
taramosalata

Serves: 6-8

Preparation time: 30'   Cooking time: no cooking required   Degree of difficulty: ❍△△   Nutritional value: △❍△
Taste: △❍△   Calories: 388

Preparation

3 slices dry bread
2 s.s. fish roe (tarama)
2 s.s. lemon juice
1 cup olive oil
2 s.s. spring onion,
finely chopped

1. Soak the bread in water, and when soft, remove the crust.
Squeeze the bread between your palms to remove most of the water.
2. Put the fish roe (tarama), lemon juice and bread which has been cut into small pieces into the blender. Beat the mixture well, add the oil in small doses. Finally add the spring onions (shallots).

Alternative: You can eliminate the bread if you want the taramosalata to feel like mayonnaise, but care is needed when you pour in the oil, as it must be poured in drop by drop at the beginning so as not to curdle the mixture.

EGGPLANT & ZUCCHINI ROLLS WITH CHEESE STUFFING

rola apo melitzana ke kolokithia me gemisi tiriou

Serves: 8-10
Preparation time: 40'   Cooking time: -   Degree of difficulty: △△⚫   Nutritional value: △⚫△
Taste: △⚫△   Calories: 323

Preparation

½ kg. (1.1 lb.) oblong eggplants
½ kg. (1.1 lb.) large zucchini
200 gr. (7 oz.) grated feta cheese
150 gr. (5.3 oz.) Philadelphia type cheese
4 s.s. chopped basil
½ cup olive oil
salt and pepper

1. Cut the eggplant and zucchini into thin slices and sprinkle with salt.
2. Place the zucchini slices on a towel to absorb their liquids.
3. Place the salted eggplant into a bowl for approximately ½ hour and then rinse with plenty of water to alleviate their bitterness and squeeze them in your hands to strain.
4. Spread out grease wrapping paper on a pan, place the eggplant and zucchini slices on it, coat them with oil and grill them on both sides for approximately 10', or until they brown.
5. Mix the remaining ingredients, while adding 2-3 tablespoons oil, and place a little of the mixture on each slice.
6. Roll each slice and serve.

GRILLED PEPPERS WITH FETA CHEESE
piperies psites me feta

Serves: 8-10

Preparation time: 20′   Cooking time: 15′   Degree of difficulty: △❍△   Nutritional value: △❍△
Taste: △△❍   Calories: 256

Preparation

10 long green peppers
300 gr. (10.6 oz.)
grated feta cheese
½ cup olive oil and
4 s.s. more pepper

1. Remove a slice from the top part of each pepper, where the stalk is, and remove the seeds.
2. Mix the cheese with 2 tablespoons olive oil and sprinkle with pepper.
3. Stuff the peppers with this mixture and replace the slice you removed earlier, onto the pepper.
4. Spread out grease wrapping paper on a pan, place the stuffed peppers on top, coat them with oil and grill them for approximately 15′, or until they brown, turning them every so often on all sides so they cook evenly.

VINE LEAVES STUFFED WITH RICE & ZUCCHINI
dolmadakia gialantzi

Serves: 8-10

Preparation time: 45′   Cooking time: 30′   Degree of difficulty: △△❍   Nutritional value: ❍△△
Taste: △❍△   Calories: 440

Preparation

½ kg. (1.1 lb.) vine leaves
15 zucchini flowers (optional)
2 cups rice
2 cups grated onion
2 grated zucchinis
5 s.s. chopped spearmint
2-3 s.s. lemon juice
1 lemon in round slices
1 cup olive oil
salt and pepper

1. Scald the vine leaves in boiling water, dipping a few at a time for 2′-3′.
2. Boil the onions in a little water and salt until they are tender and the water evaporates. Add half of the oil and sauté for a few minutes, until lightly brown.
3. Remove the onions from the heat and mix with the zucchinis, mint, rice, salt and pepper.
4. Place a teaspoon of filling on each vine leaf and roll. Also stuff the zucchini flowers.
5. Lay out some vine leaves on the bottom of a pot and place the stuffed vine leaves in a circular fashion in layers, placing the lemon slices here and there and ending with the stuffed zucchini flowers.
6. Add 3 cups warm water, the lemon juice, the remaining oil, salt and pepper and cover with a dish, so that while boiling, the stuffed vine leaves will remain in their place.
7. Cook the food at a medium heat until all the water evaporates, try it and if the rice isn't well cooked, add a little more water.

Note: The grated zucchini makes the filling juicier.

Yoghurt, Cucumber & Garlic Dip
tzatziki

Serves: 6-8

Preparation time: 5'   Cooking time: no cooking required   Degree of difficulty: ❍△△   Nutritional value: △❍△
Taste: △△❍   Calories: 200

Preparation

500 gr. (1.1 lb.)
strained yoghurt
1 cucumber, coarsely grated
3-4 mashed garlic cloves
that has been liquidized
5 s.s. olive oil
3 s.s. anise or mint,
finely chopped (optional)
salt and pepper

1. Put the grated cucumber into a thin cloth (tulle or gauze) and then place the cloth into a sieve. Add salt, mix and allow to drain for about 15'.
2. Squeeze the cucumber inside the cloth until all the liquid is removed, leaving only a compact mass.
3. Put in a bowl and add all the remaining ingredients, stirring continuously. Place in the fridge for at least 1 hour before serving.

Choumi
Dip with Chickpeas from the Cypriat Cuisine
choummi

Serves: 8-10

Preparation time: 10'   Cooking time: 1½ hours   Degree of difficulty: ❍△△   Nutritional value: △△❍
Taste: △❍△   Calories: 300

Preparation

½ kg. (1.1 lb.)
chick peas, peeled
3-4 cloves garlic, crushed
½ cup sesame paste
1 s.s. parsley, finely chopped
4 s.s. lemon juice
4 s.s. olive oil + 1 s.s. for
garnishing
salt

1. Put the chickpeas into a bowl with water for about 12 hours until they swell. Then boil for about 1½ hours until they soften and melt.
2. Strain the chickpeas and pass through a mash mill to mash them.
3. Beat the chickpea mash in a blender together with the other ingredients, except for the parsley.
4. Put the choumous in a bowl and garnish with 1 s.s. olive oil and parsley.
5. Serve the choumous as an appetiser and accompany and with pieces of bread or pita, similar to the souvlaki pita (see the recipe "SOUVLAKIA").

EGGPLANT SALAD
melitzanosalata

Serves: 4-6
Preparation time: 30'   Cooking time: 20'-25'   Degree of difficulty: △△◔   Nutritional value: ◔△△
Taste: △△◔   Calories: 272

Preparation

½ kg. (1.1 lb.)
large flask eggplants
½ cup olive oil
2 s.s. vinegar
salt

1. Clean and wipe the eggplants without removing the stem. Grill them one by one on the charcoal or on a gas flame, turning them so they cook all over until they soften and their skin is burnt (this adds a nice flavour to the eggplant salad).

2. Fill a bowl with cold water. As soon as each eggplant is cooked, you hold it by its stalk in your one hand and slowly peel it, dipping the fingers of your other hand into the water so as not to burn your fingers.

3. Place the cleaned eggplant onto a wooden block and remove as much of the the large seeds as possible. Cut the eggplants into slices so as to cut their long fibres, and then continue to cut them into small pieces to form a puree.

4. Place into a bowl and add a little vinegar to keep the mixture from turning black.

When all the above steps have been completed, slowly add the oil, stirring continuously with a fork, and add the desired salt as well as a little vinegar.

Note: If you want the eggplant salad to be creamier, you can mash the cooked eggplants in the blender instead of cutting them with a knife. If you do not like the smoked flavour of the eggplant salad, you can bake them in the oven.

Alternatives:
(a) You can add to the eggplant salad, according to your tastes, finely chopped parsley, 1-2 crushed garlic cloves, fresh peppers or finely chopped tomato.
(b) Add only half the oil mentioned in the recipe and add a cup of mayonnaise.
(c) Add a cup of strained yoghurt to the basic recipe, and if you want, a little cumin.

TUNA DIP
dip me tono

Serves: 6-8

Preparation time: 15' Cooking time: no cooking required Degree of difficulty: ❂△△ Nutritional value: △❂△
Taste: △❂△ Calories: 278

Preparation

1 tin tuna in water
½ cup home-made
mayonnaise with olive oil
½ cup strained yoghurt
1 s.s. mustard / 1 s.s. lemon juice
2 t.s. spring onions,
finely chopped
2 t.s. anise, finely chopped
salt and pepper

1. Strain the water from the tuna.
2. Put the yoghurt, mayonnaise, mustard, lemon juice and salt and
pepper into a bowl and mix with a fork or a whisk.
Finally, add the remaining ingredients. Place in the fridge for at least 1
hour before serving.

PEPPER DIP
dip piperato

Serves: 8-10

Preparation time: 20' Cooking time: 15'-20' Degree of difficulty: ❂△△ Nutritional value: △❂△
Taste: △△❂ Calories: 258

Preparation

2 long, narrow,
red Florinais type peppers
300 gr.(10.6 oz.)feta cheese
200 gr.(7 oz.)
Philadelphia cheese
4 s.s. oil
hot peppers according
to your taste

1. Grill the peppers for 15'-20' and remove the skin and seeds
2. Cut the peppers and pass put them through a blender together with
the oil.
3. Cut the feta into pieces and add to the pepper mixture, together with
the Philadelphia cheese. If the mixture is hard, add several spoonfuls of
water. Finally, slowly add pepper while tasting the dip, thus suiting it to
your taste.

VINEGRETTE SAUCE
sauce vinegret

Serves: 6-8

Preparation time: 5' Cooking time: no cooking required Degree of difficulty: ❂△△ Nutritional value: ❂△△
Taste: ❂△△ Calories: 200

Preparation

3 s.s. vinegar (preferably balsamic)
2 s.s. mustard
6 s.s. olive oil
salt and pepper

In a bowl beat the vinegar and mustard hard with a fork, then slowly add
the oil followed by salt and pepper.

Note: Instead of vinegar you may use lemon juice. You may if you like
add 1 clove crushed garlic.

MAYONNAISE
magioneza

Serves: 8-10

Preparation time: 10'   Cooking time: no cooking required   Degree of difficulty: △❶△   Nutritional value: ❶△△

Taste: △❶△   Calories: 312

2 egg yolks
2 t.s. mustard
2 t.s. lemon or vinegar
1 3/4 cups olive oil
salt and white pepper

Preparation

1. Put the egg yolks, mustard and salt into a blender and beat for 2-3 seconds, thus mixing the ingredients just over one revolution.

2. Again switch the blender on and slowly pour in the oil so as to form a thin thread as it turns. Add alternatively the oil with the lemon juice or vinegar. Finally add the pepper.

Alternatives:

(a) Tartar Sauce: Add 1 t.s. piquant mustard, 2 s.s. dill pickle finely chopped, 2 s.s. capers, 1 s.s. spring onion (shallots) and 1 s.s. estragon to 1 cup mayonnaise.

(b) Agioli: Add 2 mashed garlic cloves to the classical recipe.

(c) Pink Mayonnaise: Add to the classical recipe 1 s.s. catsup, 1 t.s. cognac, 1 t.s. Worcestershire sauce and 5 drops Tabasco sauce.

(d) Light Mayonnaise: Mix 1 cup mayonnaise with 1 cup yoghurt.

Note: All the ingredients used must be at room temperature so that the mayonnaise does not curdle. If this happens, you can easily set it again as follows: Remove the mayonnaise from the bowl of the blender and wash the latter. In the now clean bowl put in 1 egg yolk and 1 t.s. mustard and turn the switch for 2-3 seconds. Carry on as in Step 2, but instead of oil, add the curdled mayonnaise mixture and 1 more t.s. lemon juice or vinegar. Finally, add a little more salt and pepper if needed.

MEAT BALLS IN MINI PITAS
keftedakia se mini pitoules

Serves: 8-10 (25 pieces)
Preparation time: 40'   Cooking time: 8'-10'   Degree of difficulty: ❍△△   Nutritional value: △△❍
Taste: △❍△   Calories: 65 per piece

Preparation

For the filling:
½ kg. (1.1 lb.) veal mince
½ cup grated toast
1 grated onion
1 cup carbonated water
1 egg
3 s.s. chopped parsley
1 t.s. oregano
2 s.s. olive oil, plus as much as
necessary for frying
salt and pepper
For serving:
25 Lebanese mini pitas
25 tomato slices
25 onion rings
2-4 s.s. chopped parsley

1. Mix all the ingredients together and work the mixture with your hands. Leave the mixture in the refrigerator for approximately 1 hour.
2. Mould the mixture into tiny balls and press lightly to flatten them.
3. Sauté the meatballs with the oil in a non-stick pan.
4. Open the pitas and stuff them with the meatballs, the tomatoes, the onions and the parsley.
5. Serve with a bowl of yoghurt, cucumber and garlic sauce as described in the TZATZIKI recipe.

SALTED SARDINES IN OLIVE OIL
sardeles pastes se eleolado

Serves: 10-12

Preparation time: 15′ Cooking time: no cooking required Degree of difficulty: ◑△△ Nutritional value: △△◑

Taste: △◑△ Calories: 300

Preparation

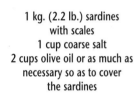

1 kg. (2.2 lb.) sardines with scales
1 cup coarse salt
2 cups olive oil or as much as necessary so as to cover the sardines

1. Spread out vine leaves in a bowl and place the sardines on them in layers, sprinkling each layer with salt. Place a vine leaf and a rock or other object on top in order to press the sardines.

2. Leave the sardines in the salt in this manner for 24 hours and then strip away their skin and cut off the heads, while removing the entrails at the same time. If you like you can remove the bone and keep only the filets.

3. Place the cleaned sardines in a bowl of oil. This way they will keep for several weeks in the refrigerator. You can serve them with a little oil and it you should accompany them with ouzo.

Note: it is essential that the sardines have scales, because otherwise they are unsuitable for preserving in salt.

Variation: a) the best sardines are considered those that are fished in and Kalloni Bay on the island of Lesvos. On the island they commonly salt sardines in the morning and they consume them at night, after 10-12 hours in salt. They serve them straight or with a little olive oil and consume them on the same day. They feel that the sardines left over are too salty to be consumed the next day!

b) Another way to keep the salted sardines from getting too salty is to place them in bags in the freezer after removing them from the salt. They are placed in the freezer for a few hours before they are consumed and they are cleaned as described in the recipe.

SALTED ANCHOVIES IN OLIVE OIL
gavros pastos se eleolado

Serves: 10-12
Preparation time: 30'   Cooking time: no cooking required   Degree of difficulty: ⬤△△   Nutritional value: △⬤△
Taste: △△⬤   Calories: 230

Preparation

1 kg. (2.2 lb.) fresh,
hard anchovies
1 cup coarse salt
2 cups vinegar or as much as
necessary to cover the anchovies
2 cups olive oil or as much as
necessary to cover the anchovies
4-5 sliced garlic cloves
5 s.s. chopped parsley
1 grated carrot
1 chopped pepper
pepper

1. Wash the fish well and cut off the heads, while at the same time removing the entrails. Place them in a bowl in layers, sprinkling salt over each layer.
2. Pour vinegar over them and let the anchovies stay like this for 10 hours. It depends on the size of the fish whether they need to stay for more hours. In order to try them to see if they're ready, open a fish and if the meat is white and the blood is gone, the fish are ready.
3. Remove the anchovies from the vinegar and remove the bones, so as to have fish filets.
4. Place the cleaned anchovies into a bowl with the remaining ingredients and fill the bowl with oil. They will keep like this in the refrigerator for several weeks.

FRIED CHEESE PIES
giuslemedes

Serves: 8-10

Preparation time: 40'   Cooking time: 30'   Degree of difficulty: △◐△   Nutritional value: △◐△
Taste: △◐△   Calories: 421

Preparation

For the pastry sheet:
½ kg. (1.1 lb.) flour
1 egg / ½ cup water
2 s.s. olive oil and
as much as needed for frying
1 t.s salt
For the filling:
2 cups grated feta cheese
1 cup grated,
unsalted mizithra cheese
1 cup grated graviera cheese
2 eggs / pepper

1. Work all the ingredients for the pastry sheets together, so that the dough becomes pliable and let it rest for ½ hour, covered.
2. In a bowl, mix all the ingredients for the filling.
3. Roll the dough until it's a thin sheet and cut.
4. Place several soupspoons of the filling onto the dough pieces, wet the ends with a little water and fold in an envelope-like manner.
5. Fry the cheese pies in hot olive oil and serve immediately.

Note: Giuslemedes are one of the aperitifs that are common in Lesvos. They make them as big as a fruit dish, and in older times, as big as the bottom of the frying pan, like pita.

FRIED CHALOUMI CHEESE
From the Cypriat Cuisine
chaloumi saganaki

Serves: 4-6

Preparation time: 5' Cooking time: 5'-7' Degree of difficulty: ◐△△   Nutritional value: △◐△
Taste: △△◐   Calories: 343

300 gr. (10.6 oz.) sliced
chaloumi cheese
enough flour to flour the
cheese slices
pepper / ½ lemon
olive oil for frying

Preparation

1. Flour the cheese slices and fry them in hot oil.
2. Place the fried chaloumi cheese on a small platter, sprinkle with pepper and squeeze a little lemon over it. Serve the cheese immediately, with fried bread slices.

Variation: The flour creates a nice, crunchy crust on the cheese when fried; you can however fry it without flouring. You can also cover the chaloumi cheese slices with a little oil (without flouring them), grill them and sprinkle with oregano and instead of pepper.

OLIVE PATE
pate elias

Serves: 6-8
Preparation time: 5′   Cooking time: no cooking required   Degree of difficulty: ⬤△△   Nutritional value: △△⬤
Taste: △△⬤   Calories: 183

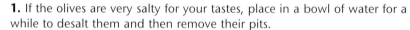

Preparation

250 gr. (8.8 oz.) black olives, not very salty
1 mashed garlic clove, liquidized
1 t.s. oregano
4-5 s.s. olive oil

1. If the olives are very salty for your tastes, place in a bowl of water for a while to desalt them and then remove their pits.
2. Put the olives, garlic and olive oil into the blender and beat until they become uniform. Then add the oregano.
3. Serve the olive pâté onto slices of slightly toasted bread as an appetiser or as a sauce for boiled potatoes and other vegetables.

Alternatives:
(a) Tapenad: This is a spicy pâté ideal for appetisers with ouzo or tsipouro. From the basic recipe for pâté exclude oregano and in its place add 2 s.s. capers, 40 gr. (1.4 oz.) anchovy fillets and 1 s.s. lemon juice. Beat all the ingredients in the blender to liquify them.
(b) You can replace the olive oil with homemade mayonnaise that has been prepared with olive oil and oregano with 2 t.s. finely chopped parsley.

CROSTETI
Grilled Bread Slices with Olive Oil
crosteti

Serves: 4-8

Preparation time: 10'   Cooking time: 8'   Degree of difficulty: ❍△△   Nutritional value: △❍△
Taste: △❍△   Calories: 360 per slice

Preparation

8 slices of bread
8 s.s. olive oil
2 t.s. oregano
salt and pepper

1. Grill or barbecue the bread.
2. Sprinkle with the olive oil, the oregano, salt and pepper.
3. Serve immediately, while the bread slices are still warm.

Note: These appetizers are prepared easily and quickly, with ingredients that can be found in any refrigerator. They are a variation of the Cretan Dakos, where in place of the rusk they use a slice of grilled, traditional Greek bread, sprinkled with salt and olive oil.

Variations: You can add to the bread slices:
a) Cubed, peeled and seedless tomatoes, capers, garlic slices sautéed in olive oil
b) sliced feta cheese, sliced tomatoes, onion rings, basil leaves
c) tinned tuna pieces, red and yellow pepper pieces, finely chopped parsley
d) small, tinned mushrooms, pitted olives, finely chopped red pepper, finely chopped parsley
e) anchovy filets, red pepper, green pepper, onion rings

FETA CHEESE DIP
dip me tiri feta

Serves: 4-6

Preparation time: 5'   Cooking time: no cooking required   Degree of difficulty: ❍△△   Nutritional value: △❍△
Taste: △❍△   Calories: 270

Preparation

150 gr.(5.3 oz.) feta cheese
250 gr.(8.8 oz.)
strained yoghurt
4 s.s. olive oil
1 s.s. grated onion
1 s.s. parsley, finely chopped

Cut the feta cheese into pieces and then put all the ingredients into the bowl of a mixer, and beat until the mixture is smooth.

RUSKS FROM CRETE
kritikos dakos

Serves: 4

Preparation time: 10'   Cooking time: no cooking required   Degree of difficulty: ❶△△   Nutritional value: △❶△
Taste: △❶△   Calories: 360

Preparation

4 round barley rusks,
called dakos in Crete
2 minced tomatoes
4 s.s. olive oil
150 gr. (5.3 oz.) feta cheese,
cut in small pieces
oregano / salt and pepper

1. Wet the rusks with a little water, pour olive oil over them and sprinkle with salt.
2. Place the tomatoes and the feta cheese on top and sprinkle with a little oregano and pepper.

OLIVE PIES
From the Cypriat Cuisine
eliopites

Serves: 10-12

Preparation time: 30'   Cooking time: 30'   Degree of difficulty: △❶△   Nutritional value: △△❶
Taste: △❶△   Calories: 473

Preparation

For the dough:
5 cups flour
2 t.s. baking powder or 1 ½ t.s.
yeast powder
1 cup water or orange juice
1 cup olive oil / 1 t.s. salt
For the filling:
1 cup minced black
or green olives
1 cup onion, finely chopped
1 t.s. mint, finely chopped
2 s.s. olive oil
salt and pepper

1. Work the flour, the baking powder and the oil together, add the salt and knead with the water or the orange juice. Allow the dough to rest for approximately 30'.
2. Sauté the onion in the oil and add the olives. Add the mint, the salt and pepper.
3. Roll out the dough into thin sheets of approximately 5 ml thickness into an oblong shape.
4. Spread the olive mixture on one edge of the pastry sheet and shape into a roll.
5. Bake the olive pies at 180° C for approximately half an hour, until brown and serve them sliced.

Note: Instead of rolling out the dough into sheets, you can knead it with the olive mixture and form small rolls.

STUFFED BABY TOMATOES
domatinia me gemisi tiriou

Serves: 10

Preparation time: 30'   Cooking time: no cooking required   Degree of difficulty: ❍△△   Nutritional value: △❍△
Taste: ❍△△   Calories: 32 per piece

Preparation

20 baby tomatoes
5 s.s. grated feta cheese
5 s.s. Philadelphia type cheese
2 s.s. olive oil
1 t.s. sweet paprika
salt and a few parsley leaves
for trimming

1. Cut a slice from the top of the baby tomatoes and empty out the interior. Sprinkle with a little salt and turn upside-down to strain.
2. Mix the remaining ingredients, except for the parsley, and stuff the tomatoes.
3. Garnish with the parsley leaves and leave in the refrigerator for at least an hour before serving.

CHEESE CROQUETTS
tirokroketes

Serves: 6-8
Preparation time: 30′ Cooking time: 10′ Degree of difficulty: △❂△ Nutritional value: △❂△
Taste: △❂△ Calories: 435

Preparation

400 gr. (14 oz.) grated
kefalograviera cheese
50 gr. (1.8 oz.) grated
parmesan cheese
2 eggs
2 s.s. flour
grated toast for frying
olive oil for frying
pepper

1. Mix all the cheeses, the eggs, the flour and the pepper in a bowl. Place the mixture in the refrigerator for 1 hour to harden.
2. Mould the cheese mixture into balls, cover with the grated toast and fry in hot oil. Serve the cheese croquettes warm.

CHALOUMI CHEESE PIES
From the Cypriat Cuisine
flaounes

Serves: 8-10

Preparation time: 40'   Cooking time: 30'   Degree of difficulty: △◐△   Nutritional value: △◐△
Taste: △◐△   Calories: 415

Preparation

For the dough:
500 gr. (1.1 lb.) flour
20 gr. (4.2 oz.) butter or olive oil
2 eggs / 3 t.s. baking powder
cup water / 120 gr.(4.2 oz.) sugar
beaten egg and sesame for the crust
For the filling: 500 gr. (1.1 lb.)
grated chaloumi cheese
4 eggs / 5 s.s. chopped parsley
½ cup raisins (optional)
1 s.s. sifted semolina
t.s. pounded mastic (optional)

1. Mix the flour, the baking powder and the sugar. Add the butter or oil and work it with your fingertips so that the mixture becomes crumbly. Add the eggs and water and work the dough well. Allow the dough to rest for approximately 30'.
2. In a bowl, mix all the filling ingredients together. Roll out the dough into a thickness of approximately 5 mm and cut into square pieces approximately 20 X 20 cm.
3. Place 2 tablespoons of the cheese mixture onto each piece of dough and fold the sides over the cheese, without covering all of it.
4. Coat the surface of each flaouna with the egg, beaten with 1-2 tablespoons water, and sprinkle with sesame.
5. Bake the pies at 180° C for approximately 30', until they brown.

MINCED MEAT PIES
From the Cypriat Cuisine
koupes

Serves: 10-12

Preparation time: 40'   Cooking time: 15'   Degree of difficulty: △△◐   Nutritional value: △△◐
Taste: △◐△   Calories: 497

Preparation

For the dough: 5 cups groats
cups warm water / ½ cup olive oil
1 cup flour / salt
For the filling:
½ kg. (1.1 lb.) mincemeat
3 chopped onions
1 chopped garlic clove
2 s.s. chopped parsley
1 egg white / 1 t.s. cinnamon
4 s.s. olive oil, or as much
as necessary for frying
salt and pepper

1. With your fingertips work the groats with the oil, so as to make a crumbly mixture, add the salt and water and let stand for approximately 2 hours so as to soak.
2. Sauté the onion and garlic in the oil and add the mincemeat. Stir the mixture until the mincemeat browns and add the parsley, salt, pepper and the cinnamon. Allow the mincemeat to cook and add the egg white while stirring.
3. Add the flour to the groats and work well so as to get a hard dough. Take 1 tablespoon of dough and open it in your hand, giving it an oval shape. Place 1 teaspoon mincemeat on it and wrap closed.
4. Fry the koupes in hot olive oil until they brown and serve warm with lemon.

STUFFED ZUCCHINI FLOWERS
kolokitholoulouda gemista

Serves: 6-8
Preparation time: 40' Cooking time: 10' Degree of difficulty: △△⬤ Nutritional value: △⬤△
Taste: △⬤△ Calories: 338

Preparation

25 zucchini flowers
For the filling:
1 cup grated feta cheese
½ cup grated unsalted
mizithra cheese
½ cup grated graviera cheese
2 s.s. chopped mint
1 egg / pepper
For the mash:
1 cup self-rising flour
1 cup carbonated water
2 egg whites
olive oil for frying

1. Prepare the filling by mixing all the ingredients in a bowl.
2. Prepare the mash, beating all the ingredients in a bowl with a whisk.
3. Wash the zucchini flowers and stuff with the filling mixture.
4. Close the oblong shaped flower petals so that the filling won't come out, dip into the mash and fry in hot oil.
5. Fry some onion rings, after also dipping them into the mash and serve warm, along with the zucchini flowers.

PESTO
pesto

Serves: 4-6
Preparation time: 10' Cooking time: no cooking required Degree of difficulty: ⬤△△ Nutritional value: ⬤△△
Taste: △⬤△ Calories: 230

Preparation

2 cups basil leaves
(without the stalk)
2 garlic cloves, cleaned
3 s.s. pinecones,
lightly sautéed
1/3 cup grated parmesan
1/3 cup olive oil
salt

1. Clean the basil leaves and place them between 2 towels to absorb the water.
2. Finely chop the garlic.
3. Place all the ingredients into the blender, except for the parmesan, and beat the mixture very well until it is mashed. Then add the parmesan and a little salt if needed.
4. If the pesto is not used immediately, place it into an airtight glass jar so it will not lose its aroma. It can be stored in the fridge for up to 2 weeks or in the freezer for a year.
5. Serve the pesto as a sauce with pasta or poured over slightly toasted bread as an appetiser.
Note: Basil with very large leaves should be used.

CHICKEN ROLLS
rola apo kotopoulo

Serves: 8-10
Preparation time: 30'   Cooking time: 30'   Degree of difficulty: △△◐   Nutritional value: △◐△
Taste: △◐△   Calories: 355 per roll

Preparation

4 boneless chicken breasts
4 s.s. chopped parsley
2 s.s. dry, crushed estragon
1 teaspoon dry, crushed thyme
150 gr. (5.3 oz.) Philadelphia type cheese
3 s.s. cream
1 crushed garlic clove
5-6 s.s. olive oil
salt and pepper

1. Split each chicken breast open by slicing it 3/4. Place between two sheets of grease wrapping paper and press lightly with a rolling pin in a back-and-forth motion, until the chicken breasts become flat, broad filets of uniform thickness.
2. Prepare the mixture with the cheese, the cream, the garlic, the aromatic herbs, salt and pepper.
3. Salt and pepper the chicken filets, place the cheese mixture on them and fold into rolls.
4. Coat each roll with olive oil, wrap in aluminium foil and broil at 180° C for ½ hour. Remove the aluminium foil and roast for 15' more, or until the rolls brown.
5. Allow the rolls to cool and cut into slices.

VINE LEAF & MINCEMEAT ROLLS
From the Cypriat Cuisine
koupepia

Serves: 4-6
Preparation time: 60'   Cooking time: 40'   Degree of difficulty: △△◐   Nutritional value: △◐△
Taste: △◐△   Calories: 604

Preparation

½ kg. (1.1 lb.) mixed veal and pork mincemeat
1 small cup rice
2 s.s. lemon juice
2 grated onions
2 s.s. cinnamon
1 s.s. chopped mint
1 cup cubed, peeled, seedless tomatoes
1 s.s. tomato paste diluted in 1 cup warm water
juice of 1 lemon (optional)
5 s.s. olive oil
salt and pepper
50-60 vine leaves

1. Scald the vine leaves in boiling water by dipping a few of them in at a time for 2'-3'.
2. Mix the mincemeat with one onion, the rice, the cinnamon, the mint, the tomato, salt and pepper and work in a dough-like fashion.
3. Place one teaspoon of filling on each vine leaf and roll into dolmadakia (koupepia).
4. Spread some vine leaves on the bottom of a pot and place the rolls in a circular manner and in layers.
5. Sauté the other onion in the oil and add the tomato paste, diluted in water, and pour into the pot with the rolls.
6. Cover with a dish, so as the rolls boil they will remain in their place, and add water to cover them.
7. Cook the food at a medium heat, until all the water evaporates, try it, and if the rice is not well cooked, add some more water. At the end add the lemon juice.

PUMPKIN PIE
From the Cypriat Cuisine
kolokotes

Serves: 10-12
Preparation time: 30'   Cooking time: 30' Degree of difficulty: △❍△   Nutritional value: △❍△
Taste: △❍△   Calories: 424

Preparation

For the dough:
½ kg. (1.1 lb.) flour
½ cup olive oil
½ cup water
For the filling:
1 kg. (2.2 lb.) yellow
grated pumpkin
200 gr. (7 oz.) dark raisins
150 gr. (5.3 oz.) groats
2 chopped onions
½ t.s. cinnamon (optional)
6 s.s. olive oil
1 s.s. coarse salt

1. Mix the flour with the salt and the oil and work it with your fingertips so as to make a crumbly mixture. Add the water and work the dough well. Allow the dough to rest for approximately 30'.
2. Place the grated pumpkin on a thin piece of cloth (toile, gauze or veil) and place it on a strainer, in the cloth. Add salt, stir and allow to strain for approximately 1 hour.
3. Squeeze the pumpkin in the cloth so as to strain all its liquid, leaving a compact mass.
4. Sauté the onion in the oil and add the pumpkin, the groats and the raisins. Lightly stir the mixture so as to absorb any remaining liquid.
5. Spread the dough into pastry sheets with a thickness of approximately 5 mm and cut it into round shapes with a diameter of 10-15 cm.
Place 1-2 tablespoons of the filling on each circle, fold in the middle, so as to shape a half moon, and press the edges.
6. Bake the pies at 180° C for approximately 30', until they brown.

BAKED POTATOES WITH OLIVE OIL SAUCE
patates psites me sauce apo eleolado

Serves: 10
Preparation time: 10'   Cooking time: 1 hour Degree of difficulty: ❍△△   Nutritional value: △❍△
Taste: △❍△   Calories: 210

Preparation

10 medium size potatoes
10 s.s. olive oil
1 s.s. lemon juice
4 s.s. mustard
4 s.s. cream
4 s.s. chopped parsley
salt and pepper

1. Wash the potatoes and wrap in aluminium foil. Bake at 200° C for 1 hour, or until soft.
2. Beat the remaining ingredients in a bowl.
3. Open the top part of the aluminium foil and score each potato crosswise with a knife. Add salt and pepper and pour the olive oil sauce onto it. Serve immediately, while the potatoes are still warm.

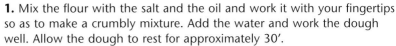

SHISH KEBAB VARIETIES
pikilia apo souvlakia

Serves: 8-10

Preparation time: 30'   Cooking time: 10'   Degree of difficulty: ❂△△   Nutritional value: △❂△
Taste: △❂△   Calories: 80 (per 100gr.)

500 gr. (1.1 lb.) boneless chicken breast cut into ribbons
500 gr. (1.1 lb.) pork cut into ribbons
500 gr. (1.1 lb.) large, shrimps, without the shell
50 gr. (1.8 oz.) sesame
For the marinade:
1 small, grated onion
2 crushed garlic cloves
½ t.s. chilli
2 s.s. grated ginger
3 s.s. soy sauce
2 s.s. balsam vinegar
4 s.s. olive oil

Preparation

1. Place the various kebab pieces into a bowl, mix the marinade ingredients well and pour over the kebab pieces. Put the basin in the refrigerator and leave for 3-10 hours.
2. Skewer the kebab pieces and sprinkle with the sesame.
3. Rub oil on the grill, place the shish kebabs on it and grill or barbecue them for approximately 5'-10', or until brown. Serve with fresh vegetables and various dips.

STUFFED MUSHROOMS
manitaria gemista

Serves: 8-10

Preparation time: 20'   Cooking time: 10'-15'   Degree of difficulty: ❂△△   Nutritional value: △❂△
Taste: ❂△△   Calories: 52 per piece

Preparation

20 fresh, large mushrooms
1 grated onion
10 s.s. grated kefalograviera cheese
2 s.s. cream
2 s.s. parsley
4 s.s. olive oil
salt and pepper

1. Remove the stems from the mushrooms and chop.
2. Sauté the onion in olive oil, add the mushrooms stems, salt and pepper and simmer until the liquids evaporate.
3. Add the cream, remove the mixture from the heat and add the cheese and the parsley.
4. Stuff the mushrooms with this mixture, place in a pan, coat with a little oil and broil at 180°C for 10'-15'.

PICKLED TINY EGGPLANTS
melitzanakia toursi

Serves: 10-12

Preparation time: 45'   Cooking time: 5'   Degree of difficulty: △△◐   Nutritional value: ◐△△
Taste: △△◐   Calories: 140

Preparation

1 kg. (2.2 lb.) tiny eggplants
1 cup shredded carrot
1 cup chopped red pepper
6-7 chopped garlic cloves
1 cup chopped parsley
½ kg. (1.1 lb.) celery
3 cups vinegar
as much olive oil
as necessary to fill the jar

1. Wash the eggplants, cut their stems and carve them.
2. Scald them for 5' in boiling water, strain them and place them in pickling brine, which you will prepare as follows: in 1 litre boiling water pour 100gr. (3.5 oz.) coarse salt and stir to dilute it. Let it cool and put an egg in it. If the egg rises to the surface and a coin-size part of the egg emerges from the water, the brine is ready. If the egg doesn't rise to the surface, the brine needs more salt. Place the eggplants in the pickling brine for 24 hours.
3. Stir the carrot, pepper, garlic and parsley and fill the eggplants in the groove you made.
4. Scald the celery for 5' in boiling water and tie each eggplant all around with a celery stalk.
5. Place the eggplants in a bowl with a cover, pour the vinegar over them, after boiling it for 2'-3', and cover the bowl.
6. Let the eggplants stay in the vinegar for 1 week and then place them in a sterilized glass jar, cover them with oil and close the jar. In a week they are ready to be consumed.

Note: you can find tiny eggplants in the market only during the beginning of Autumn.

SUN-DRIED TOMATOES IN OLIVE OIL
domates liastes se eleolado

Serves: 8-10

Preparation time: 15'   Cooking time: no cooking required   Degree of difficulty: ❶△△   Nutritional value: ❶△△
Taste: △❶△   Calories: 115

Preparation

2 cups olive oil
10 small tomatoes
2 garlic cloves
1 t.s. thyme, basil, oregano
2 s.s. vinegar, preferably balsam
coarse salt

1. Wash and dry the tomatoes. Cut them in two, lengthwise, and place them on paper towels to strain their liquid. Sprinkle them with the salt. Approximately 1/3 teaspoon of salt will be required for each piece.
2. Place the tomatoes on a straw or wooden surface, with the cut side on top, cover them with a cloth (toile, gauze or veil) so they won't get dusty, and leave them in the sun. They will need to stay there for approximately 10 days or more, until all their liquids dry out and they shrivel.
3. Place the dry tomatoes in a pan and sprinkle them with a little vinegar.
4. Place the tomatoes into a sterilized glass jar with a screw-on cover, as follows: put in a layer of tomatoes, sprinkle with the condiments and the chopped garlic and pour oil over them. Continue in the same fashion until all the ingredients are used and pour as much oil as is needed to completely cover the tomatoes in the jar.
5. Close the jar well and keep it in a dark, cool place. They keep in this way for a fairly long time. After opening the jar, place it in the refrigerator.

Note: You can alternately dry the tomatoes in the oven. Place them with the cut part on top, after having placed them, in accordance with step 1 above, in a pan on which you will have spread aluminium foil and roast in a pre-warmed oven at 90°C for approximately 8 hours. The tomatoes will be ready when all their liquids have evaporated. Let them cook and continue with steps 3, 4 and 5, as for the sun-dried tomatoes.

PICKLED ARTICHOKES
aginares toursi

Serves: 10-12
Preparation time: 60′   Cooking time: 5′   Degree of difficulty: △❍△   Nutritional value: ❍△△
Taste: ❍△△   Calories: 120

Preparation

1 kg. (2.2 lb.) artichoke hearts
1 lemon
75 ml. dry white wine
25 ml. vinegar
1 s.s. black, granulated pepper
1 t.s. cloves
as much olive oil as necessary
to fill the jar
salt

1. Clean the artichokes, removing the stalks, the tough leaves and the fuzz from their interior and rub them with a little lemon juice to prevent them from darkening.
2. Place the cleaned artichokes in a bowl with a little water, enough to cover them, in which you will have added the juice of 1 lemon.
3. Put the wine, vinegar, 1 tablespoon salt, 2 clove spikes, some pepper grains and 2 bay leaves in a pot and cook for 5′.
4. Remove the pot from the heat and add the artichokes. Leave them there until the vinegar cools and place them in sterilized glass jars.
5. Place 1 bay leaf, some pepper grains and cloves in each jar and fill with oil.
6. Close the jars well and place them in the refrigerator. In 2-3 days the artichokes are ready to consume.

PICKLED ONIONS
kremidakia toursi

Serves: 10-12
Preparation time: 15′   Cooking time: 5′   Degree of difficulty: ❍△△   Nutritional value: ❍△△
Taste: △❍△   Calories: 132

Preparation

1 kg. (2.2 lb.) small onions
1 cup coarse salt
½ litre vinegar
30 gr. (1.5 oz.) sugar
1 t.s. pepper grains
1 t.s. cloves
as much olive oil as necessary
to fill the jar

1. Clean the onions and sprinkle with the salt. Let them stand like this overnight and then wash and strain them.
2. Scald them for 5′ in boiling vinegar and then remove the pot from the heat. Leave the onions in the hot vinegar until the vinegar cools.
3. Fill a sterilized jar with the onions, pour the olive oil in it and close the jar well. In 2-3 days they are ready to be consumed.

PICKLED EGGPLANTS IN OLIVE OIL
melitzanes toursi se eleolado

Serves: 10-12

Preparation time: 15' Cooking time: 4' Degree of difficulty: ❖△△ Nutritional value: ❖△△
Taste: △△❖ Calories: 165

Preparation

1 kg. (2.2 lb.) eggplants
4 garlic cloves
4 small hot peppers
4 s.s. chopped parsley
1 cup vinegar
olive oil, as much as needed
to fill the jar

1. Cut the eggplants into slices and sprinkle them with salt. Allow to stand for 4-5 hours and then strain them, squeezing them in your hands.
2. Scald the eggplants for 4' in 1 litre boiling water in which you've added the vinegar. Remove them and place them on an absorbent paper towel to strain.
3. Place them in a sterilized glass jar with the other ingredients and close the jar well. In 3-4 weeks they are ready to be consumed.

PICKLED MUSHROOMS IN OLIVE OIL
manitaria toursi se eleolado

Serves: 6-8

Preparation time: 15' Cooking time: 1' Degree of difficulty: ❖△△ Nutritional value: ❖△△
Taste: ❖△△ Calories: 150

Preparation

500 gr. (1.1 lb.) mushrooms
without stems
3/4 cup olive oil
1/4 cup vinegar
with estragon aroma
1/4 cup chopped parsley
1 chopped garlic clove
salt and granulated pepper

1. Scald the mushrooms for 1' in salted, boiling water. Strain them and place in a sterilized glass jar.
2. Mix the other ingredients and place in the jar with the mushrooms.
3. Close the jar well and place in the refrigerator. In two days the mushrooms are ready to be consumed.

POUNDED OLIVES WITH CORIANDER
elies tsakistes me koliandro

Serves: 4-6

Preparation time: 5' Cooking time: no cooking required Degree of difficulty: ❖△△ Nutritional value: △❖△
Taste: △❖△ Calories: 160

Preparation

cup pounded, green, debittered
olives, ready to eat (see how to
ebitter olives in the introduction)
2 chopped cloves of garlic
1 t.s. pounded coriander
2 s.s. olive oil
2 s.s. lemon juice
lemon slices

Mix all the ingredients and serve in a bowl, garnishing with the lemon slices.

PICKLED PEPPERS
piperies toursi

Serves: 8-10

Preparation time: 15' Cooking time: 15' Degree of difficulty: ❶△△ Nutritional value: ❶△△
Taste: △△❶ Calories: 120

Preparation

½ kg. (1.1 lb.) red, long peppers, Florina type
100 gr. (3.5 oz.) celery
1 sliced onion
4 garlic cloves
1 cup vinegar
½ cup olive oil
salt and grainy pepper

1. Grill the peppers on both sides for 15' or until they brown.
2. Peel them, cut off the stems and remove the seeds.
3. Boil the vinegar with the celery, the onion, the garlic and the salt for 5' and strain, without discarding the vinegar.
4. Place a layer of peppers in an oblong bowl with a cover, and sprinkle part of the onions, the garlic the pepper and the chopped celery over them. Continue in this fashion until all the ingredients are used, pour the vinegar and oil over them and close the bowl well.
5. Keep the peppers in the refrigerator. They are ready to be consumed in approximately 2 weeks.

FETA CHEESE IN OLIVE OIL
tiri feta se eleolado

Serves: 8-10

Preparation time: 5' Cooking time: no cooking required Degree of difficulty: ❶△△ Nutritional value: △❶△
Taste: △❶△ Calories: 275

Preparation

½ kg. (1.1 lb.) hard feta cheese (preferably teleme cheese)
2-3 twigs rosemary
1 t.s. black pepper
1 t.s. coriander
2 cups olive oil

1. Slice the cheese in 2cm. width slices.
2. Place the cheese slices in a glass bowl (they can be found in the market in square shapes, with plastic, airtight covers) and add the rosemary, the pepper and the coriander.
3. Fill the bowl with olive oil, enough to cover the slices of cheese, close the bowl well and keep it in the refrigerator.
4. Serve the feta cheese by placing a slice on a small dish. Pour 1-2 tablespoons oil on it, as well as freshly ground pepper.

LADOTYRI CHEESE IN OLIVE OIL
ladotiri se eleolado

Serves: 14-16

Preparation time: 10'   Cooking time: no cooking required   Degree of difficulty: ⚫△△   Nutritional value: △⚫△
Taste: △⚫△   Calories: 350

Preparation

1 head of ladotyri cheese,
approximately 1 kg. (2.2 lb.)
1 ½ kg. (3,3 lb.) olive oil
1 t.s. oregano

1. Slice the ladotyri cheese, sprinkle with oregano and place in a sterilized jar with a screw-on cover.
2. Fill the jar with olive oil until the cheese slices are covered, close the jar well and keep it in a dark and cool place. After opening the jar, it must be kept in the refrigerator.

Note: The ladotyri cheese is a typical, regional product of Lesvos, in the shape of a small head, which owes its name to the fact that it was preserved in oil, which was the only traditional way to preserve it in the past when there were no refrigerators. Today the cheese is covered in a paraffin layer and is kept in the refrigerator. For this reason, you must remove the paraffin with a knife, before putting it in oil. The oil in which the ladotyri is preserved can be reused for the same reason, but no more than twice, because it then becomes tangy.

Pies

pites

SPINACH PIE

spanakopita

Serves: 10-12

Preparation time: 40' Cooking time: 40'-50' Degree of difficulty: △❶△ Nutritional value: △△❶

Taste: △❶△ Calories: 336

Preparation

1 kg. (2,.2 lb.) spinach
5 spring onions, finely chopped
2 leeks, finely chopped
2 s.s. anise, finely chopped
250 gr. (8.8 oz.) feta cheese cut into small pieces
2 s.s. frumenty (trachana) or semolina
2/3 cup olive oil
salt and pepper
For the pastry sheets
½ kg. (1,.1 lb.) flour
2 s.s. olive oil
1 cup lukewarm water
1 s.s. vinegar
1 t.s. salt

1. Clean and wash the spinach, then cut it into small pieces. Put them into a thin cloth (tulle or gauze) and then place the cloth into a sieve. Add salt, mix and allow to drain for about 15'.

2. Squeeze the spinach inside the cloth until all the liquid is removed, leaving only a compact mass.

3. Sauté the spring onions (shallots) and the leeks with 4-5 s.s. oil, add the spinach and stir the mixture so as to absorb all the remaining liquid.

4. Remove the mixture from the fire, allow to cool and then add the anise, the cheese, the frumenty and the pepper. Do not add any more salt because you have salted the spinach and have added cheese, so the mixture therefore has all the salt it needs.

5. To prepare the pastry sheets, sift the flour into a bowl, make a hole in the middle and add 3/4 of the water and the remaining ingredients. Knead the flour little-by-little for about 15', adding the remaining water if needed. The dough must be smooth, not very hard and easily moulded without it sticking to the hands. Add a little more flour if needed. If the dough is a little too hard, wet your fingers and knead until the dough softens. If it is too soft, add a little more flour.
Separate the dough into 6 balls, cover with a towel and allow the dough to "sit" for 1 hour. Roll out the dough balls into thin sheets on a floured surface. To lay out the sheets in the pan, transport them rolled up on the rolling pin.

6. Oil a baking pan or dish and lay out half the pastry sheets, coating each one with oil. Spread out the filling and cover with the remaining pastry sheets, coating each one with oil.

7. Cut the pie into slices without reaching the bottom of the dish, sprinkle a little water and bake at 180oC for about 40'-50' until the pie browns.

Note: If you do not want to make the dough yourself, you may use ready-made kourou, vergas or choriatiko dough

Yellow Pumpkin Pie

kolokithopita me kitrini kolokitha

Serves: 10-12

Preparation time: 30'   Cooking time: 40'-50'   Degree of difficulty: △❍△   Nutritional value: △❍△
Taste: △❍△   Calories: 393

Preparation

2 kourou pastry sheets
(ready-made)
1 kg. (2.2 lb.)
yellow pumpkin
2 onions, finely chopped
200 gr. (7 oz.)
grated feta cheese
100 gr. (3.5 oz.) grated
kefalogavriera cheese
4 eggs / 2 s.s. mint,
finely chopped (optional)
2 s.s. frumenty (trachana)
or semolina
2 s.s. grounded nutmeg
2/3 cup olive oil / salt and pepper

1. Clean the pumpkin and grate it on a large grater. Put the grated pumpkin into a thin cloth (tulle or gauze) and then place the cloth into a sieve. Add salt, mix and allow to drain for about 15'.
2. Squeeze the pumpkin inside the cloth until all the liquid is removed, leaving only a compact mass.
3. Sauté the onion with 3-4 s.s. oil, add the pumpkin and stir the mixture until all the remaining liquid has been absorbed.
4. Remove the mixture from the fire, allow to cool a little and add the cheeses, eggs that have been beaten, the mint, the frumenty (trachana), the nutmeg and the pepper. No additional salt is needed because you have already salted the pumpkin and added the cheeses, so the mixture therefore has all the salt it needs.
5. Oil a baking pan or dish and put in a pastry sheet. Spread the filling on the sheet and cover with the second pastry sheet which has been coated with milk.
6. Cut the pie into slices without reaching the bottom of the dish and bake at 180° C for about 40'-50' until it browns.

Note: You can replace the yellow pumpkin with a green one.
The frumenty (trachanas) is added to the mixture in order to absorb the additional liquids. It may be replaced by semolina or even coarsely grounded toast.

CHEESE PIE
tiropita

Serves: 10-12

Preparation time: 30'   Cooking time: 30'-40'   Degree of difficulty: ❍△△   Nutritional value: △△❍
Taste: △❍△   Calories: 412

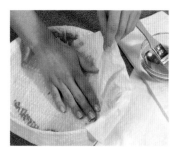  

Preparation

½ kg. (1,.1 lb.) pie crust
300 gr. (10.6 oz.) grated feta cheese
200 gr. (7 oz.) grated Naxos or Cretan "sweet" gruyere cheese
4 eggs
1 cup milk
2/3 cup olive oil
½ t.s. grounded nutmeg and pepper

1. Mix the cheeses
2. Oil a baking pan or dish with a little oil and put in 2-3 pastry sheets, coating each one with oil.
3. Sprinkle a little of the cheese mix, cover with a pastry sheet and tuck it in, then coat with a little oil. Repeat until the ingredients are finished, ending with the cheese mix. Do not press the pastry sheets in order to leave an opening between the layers, thus giving the pie a fluffy look. Make sure to keep 3 sheets for the top part of the pie.
4. Beat the eggs with the milk in a bowl and add the nutmeg and pepper.
Pour this mixture over the cheese pie and finish up by adding the 3 last pastry sheets that you had kept, coating each one with a little oil.
5. Cut the pie into slices without reaching the bottom of the dish, sprinkle a little water and bake at 180° C for about 40'-50' until the pie browns.

MEATLOAF PIE
kreatopita rolo

Serves: 10-12
Preparation time: 30'   Cooking time: 30'-40'   Degree of difficulty: △❍△   Nutritional value: △△❍
Taste: △❍△   Calories: 446

Preparation

½ kg. (1,.1 lb.) pie crust
½ kg. (1,.1 lb.) veal mince
2 large onions, finely chopped
2 garlic cloves, finely chopped
2 egg whites
4 eggs boiled and cut into pieces
150 gr. (5.3 oz.) grated
kefalogavriera cheese
2 s.s parsley
2 t.s. Soya sauce
½ t.s. cinnamon
2 t.s. paprika
2 s.s. grated toast
2/3 cup olive oil
salt and pepper

1. Sauté the onion and the garlic with 4-5 s.s. oil and when brown, add the mincemeat. Sauté a little until the mincemeat browns and all the liquid has been absorbed, then add the remaining ingredients.
2. Roll out the dough onto a level surface, the one on top of the other, coating each one with oil.
3. Spread out the mincemeat on the pastry sheets, covering 3/4 surfaces.
4. Wrap up into a roll, coat with oil and bake at 180° C for about 40'-45' until it browns. Allow the meat pie to cool a little and then cut the roll into slices.

Fresh Tomato & Feta Cheese Pizza

pitsa me freskia domata ke feta

Serves: 8-10

Preparation time: 15' Cooking time: 20' Degree of difficulty: ❍△△ Nutritional value: △❍△
Taste: △❍△ Calories: 282

Preparation

For the dough:
250 gr. (8.8 oz.) flour
15 gr. (0,5 oz.) yeast
10 s.s. lukewarm water
2 s.s. olive oil / salt
For the filling:
3 tomatoes in round slices
2 cups feta cheese
cut in small pieces
10 minced olives,
without the pits
5 s.s. olive oil / oregano

1. Knead all the dough ingredients, after dissolving the yeast in water, until the dough becomes soft and pliable. If needed, add a little more lukewarm water.

2. Cover the dough with a plastic wrap and let it rest for approximately 15-20' minutes.

3. Spread the dough in a round shape and place in an oiled pan.

4. Coat the dough surface with oil, and cover with the tomato slices, the cheese and the olives.

5. Pour the remaining olive oil on the pizza, sprinkle with oregano and bake at 300°C for approximately 15-20'.

Note: You can use ready-made dough from the bakery or supermarket.

Leek Pie

prasopita

Serves: 10-12

Preparation time: 30' Cooking time: 40'-50' Degree of difficulty: △❍△ Nutritional value: △❍△
Taste: △❍△ Calories: 382

Preparation

½ kg. (1.1 lb.) pie crust
1 kg. (2.2 lb.) leeks,
finely chopped
3-4 s.s. anise, finely chopped
4 eggs
250 gr. (8.8 oz.) feta cheese
cut into small pieces
2 s.s. frumenty (trachana)
or semolina
2/3 cup olive oil
salt and pepper

1. Boil the leeks in water and a little salt until tender and all the water evaporates (take care not to salt them too much because when you add the cheese, the mixture will be too salty).

2. Put 4-5 tablespoons oil in the pot with the leeks and sauté for a few minutes, until they are lightly brown.

3. Pull the pot from the fire and when the leeks cool, add the anise, the eggs, the cheese, the frumenty and the pepper.

4. Oil a baking pan or fire resistant dish and lay out half the pastry sheets, coating each one with oil. Spread out the filling and cover with the remaining pastry sheets, coating each one with oil.

5. Cut the pie into slices without reaching the bottom of the dish, sprinkle a little water and bake at 180°C for about 40'-50' until the pie browns.

WILD GREENS PIE
chortopita

Serves: 10-12

Preparation time: 50'   Cooking time: 40'-50'   Degree of difficulty: △●△   Nutritional value: ●△△
Taste: △●△   Calories: 280

Preparation

½ kg. (1.1 lb.) various wild greens: wild chicory (radikia), sow thistle (zochi), endives (antidia), etc.
100 gr. (3.5 oz.) kafkalithres (wild greens with an intense aroma) or fennel (maratho)
½ kg. (1.1 lb.) spinach
2 cups leeks, finely chopped
1 cup spring onions, finely chopped
4 s.s. anise
2 s.s. frumenty (trachana) or semolina / 2/3 cup olive oil
Dough for pastry sheets, as described in the recipe "SPINACH PIE", or kourou, vergas or choriatiko.

1. Clean and wash the spinach, then cut it into small pieces. Put them into a thin cloth (tulle or gauze) and then place the cloth into a sieve. Add salt, mix and allow to drain for about 15'.

2. Squeeze the spinach inside the cloth until all the liquid is removed, leaving only a compact mass. Wash the various wild greens and chop finely.

3. Sauté the spring onions (shallots) and the leeks with 6 s.s. oil, add the spinach and the wild greens and stir the mixture so as to absorb all the remaining liquid.

4. Remove the mixture from the fire, allow to cool and then add the anise, the frumenty, salt and pepper.

5. Oil a baking pan or dish and lay out half the pastry sheets, coating each one with oil. Spread out the filling and cover with the remaining pastry sheets, coating each one with oil.

6. Cut the pie into slices without reaching the bottom of the dish, sprinkle a little water and bake at 180° C for about 40'-50' until the pie browns.

EGGPLANT PIE
melitzanopita

Serves: 10-12

Preparation time: 30'   Cooking time: 40'-50'   Degree of difficulty: △●△   Nutritional value: △●△
Taste: △●△   Calories: 425

Preparation

2 puff pastry sheets (ready-made)
750 gr. (1.65 lb.) eggplants
300 gr. (10.6 oz.) mozzarella cheese cut into thin slices
½ cup milk cream
1 cup yoghurt
3 eggs
3/4 cup olive oil
salt and pepper
For the mash:
1 cup flour
1 cup water
2 egg whites
olive oil for frying

1. Cut the eggplants into slices, salt them and allow to rest for about 30' to de-bitter. Wash them and squeeze them in the palms of your hands to remove all excess liquid.

2. Prepare a mash with the flour and water and add the salt, pepper and egg whites that have been beaten. Allow the mash to "sit" for about 1 hour. Then dip the eggplant rings into it and then into the hot oil to fry.

3. Butter a baking pan or dish and place a pastry sheet in it. Put in a layer of eggplants, then some pieces of feta cheese and repeat until the ingredients have finished.

4. Cover with the other pastry sheet and cut the pie into slices without reaching the bottom of the dish.

5. Beat the eggs with the milk cream and yoghurt and pour over the pie. Bake at 180° C for about 40'-50' until the pie browns.

Note: You can replace the mozzarella with emental or other "sweet" cheese. You can also prepare the eggplant pie "uncovered"; i.e. without using the pastry sheets.

SALADS

salates

TRADITIONAL GREEK SALAD
choriatiki salata

Serves: 4

Preparation time: 15'   Cooking time: no cooking required   Degree of difficulty: ❶△△   Nutritional value: △❶△
Taste: △❶△   Calories: 300

3 tomatoes
1 small cucumber
1 sliced pepper
1 onion
½ cup olives
2 s.s. oregano
5 s.s. olive oil
1 cup feta cheese in small pieces
2 s.s. vinegar (optional) / salt

Preparation

1. Cut the tomatoes into slices, the cucumber into round slices and the onion into slices or round slices.
2. Place the vegetables into a salad bowl and mix them with the olives.
3. Add the feta cheese, pour in the oil and vinegar and sprinkle with oregano.
4. Accompany the salad with traditional Greek bread.

Variations: You can add chopped parsley, chopped rocket, glistrida gree and capers.

BEAN SALAD
fasolia salata

Serves: 4-6

Preparation time: 15'   Cooking time: 60'   Degree of difficulty: ❶△△   Nutritional value: △△❶
Taste: △❶△   Calories: 322

250 gr. (8.8 oz.) dried beans
3-4 chopped shallots
1 sliced, small pepper
3 s.s. chopped parsley
10 olives
1 salad lettuce
3 s.s. lemon juice or vinegar
2 s.s. mustard
6 s.s. olive oil
salt and pepper

Preparation

1. Put the beans into a bowl of water to puff for at least 12 hours.
2. Boil them until tender and strain them.
3. Spread the lettuce leaves out in a salad bowl and place the beans or them, after they cool and after mixing them with the shallots, the peppe the parsley, the olives, salt and pepper.
4. Beat the oil, the lemon juice, the mustard, salt and pepper in a bow and pour over the beans.

SALAD WITH ROKA & PARMESAN
salata me roka ke parmezana

Serves: 4-6

Preparation time: 10'   Cooking time: no cooking required   Degree of difficulty: ❂△△   Nutritional value: △❂△
Taste: △❂△   Calories: 282

For the salad:
1 salad lettuce
1 skein rocket
2 cups tender spinach leaves
3 s.s. chopped shallot
2 s.s. chopped anise
1/4 cup thickly grated
parmesan cheese
½ cup thickly pounded walnuts
For the dressing:
2 t.s. mustard
3 t.s. lemon juice
2 s.s. olive oil
2 s.s. mayonnaise
salt and pepper

Preparation

1. Wash the vegetables well and cut them into bite size pieces.
2. Place them in a bowl and mix them with the remaining ingredients.
3. Beat all the ingredients for the dressing and pour over the salad.

MACARONI SALAD
makaronosalata

Serves: 4

Preparation time: 25'   Cooking time: 20'   Degree of difficulty: ❂△△   Nutritional value: △△❂
Taste: △❂△   Calories: 400

For the salad:
1 salad lettuce
200 gr. (7 oz.) cooked
screw-shaped macaroni
4 anchovy filets cut in pieces
2 sliced boiled eggs
1 s.s. capers
5 s.s. thickly pounded walnuts
For the dressing:
1 garlic clove cut in half
5 s.s. olive oil
2 s.s. lemon juice
1 s.s. mayonnaise
1 t.s. mustard / pepper
2 s.s. grated parmesan

Preparation

1. Rub the garlic on the inside of the salad bowl.
2. Beat all the ingredients for the dressing.
3. Wash the lettuce, cut into large pieces and mix with the remaining ingredients of the salad.
4. Place the salad into a salad bowl with the dressing and mix. Sprinkle with the parmesan and serve immediately.

SUMMER SALAD WITH WILD GREENS
chorta vrasta salata kalokerini

Serves: 4-6
Preparation time: 15'   Cooking time: 25'   Degree of difficulty: ❍△△   Nutritional value: ❍△△
Taste: ❍△△   Calories: 260

Preparation

700 gr. (1,52 lb.) vlita
300 gr. (10.6 oz.) zucchini
½ cup olive oil
4 s.s. vinegar
salt and pepper

1. Clean the vlita, keeping the leaves and tender stems and discarding the tough stalks.
2. Cut the ends of the zucchini and scrape their surface lightly.
3. Boil the greens and the zucchini for approximately 25', as in the recipe WINTER SALAD WITH WILD GREENS, and strain them.
4. Place them in a bowl, pour the oil and vinegar over them and sprinkle with a bit of pepper.
5. Serve cold and accompany them with a garlic dip(skordalia).

POTATO SALAD
patatosalata

Serves: 4-6
Preparation time: 15'   Cooking time: 30'   Degree of difficulty: ❍△△   Nutritional value: △❍△
Taste: △❍△   Calories: 325

Preparation

For the salad:
500 gr. (1.1 lb.) potatoes
1 chopped onion
1 cubed red pepper
1 cubed green pepper
½ cup chopped,
pickled cucumbers
4 s.s. caper
5 s.s. chopped parsley
For the dressing:
1 s.s. mustard
1/3 cup olive oil / 3 s.s. vinegar

1. Boil the potatoes for approximately 30', until they are tender, skin them and cut into pieces.
2. Beat all the ingredients for the dressing and pour over the hot potatoes.
3. Add the remaining ingredients and serve the salad warm or cold.

Variation: You can replace the dressing with 1 dose mayonnaise, as described in the MAYONNAISE recipe.

GREEN VEGETABLE & SHRIMP SALAD
salata me prasina lahanika ke garides

Serves: 10
Preparation time: 20'   Cooking time: 8'   Degree of difficulty: ❍△△   Nutritional value: △❍△
Taste: ❍△△   Calories: 430

For the salad:
1 iceberg lettuce
1 endive lettuce / 1 red lettuce
1 bunch watercress / 1 chicory
5 sliced radishes
6 s.s. chopped shallot
4 s.s. chopped anise
1 kg. (2.2 lb.) boiled
and cleaned shrimp
For the dressing:
2/3 cup olive oil
8 s.s. lemon juice
salt and pepper

Preparation

1. Wash all the vegetables well and cut them into bite size pieces.
2. Place them into a bowl and mix them with the remaining ingredients.
3. Beat all the ingredients for the dressing and pour over the salad.

AVOCADO SALAD
salata me avocado

Serves: 6-8

Preparation time: 10'   Cooking time: no cooking required   Degree of difficulty: ❶△△   Nutritional value: △△❶
Taste: △❶△   Calories: 330

Preparation

For the salad: 1 salad type lettuce
1 bunch rocket
2 avocadoes / 1 red pepper
10 cherry tomatoes
the juice of 1 lemon
1 garlic clove cut in half
For the dressing:
6 s.s. olive oil / 3 t.s. vinegar
salt and pepper

1. Wash the lettuce and the rocket well and cut into bite size pieces.
2. Slice the avocado, place the slices into a bowl and sprinkle with the lemon juice so they won't darken.
3. Cut the pepper into matchstick size pieces.
4. Rub the salad bowl interior with the garlic and place the salad ingredients into it.
5. Beat all the ingredients for the dressing and pour over the salad.

GROATS SALAD
From the Cypriat Cuisine
tapouli

Serves: 4-6

Preparation time: 15'   Cooking time: no cooking required   Degree of difficulty: ❶△△   Nutritional value: △△❶
Taste: △❶△   Calories: 330

1 cup groats
5 s.s. chopped parsley
5 s.s. chopped mint
1 chopped onion
1 cup cubed, peeled, seedless tomatoes
1 cup cucumber cut into small pieces
6 s.s. olive oil
the juice of 2 lemons / salt and pepper

Preparation

1. Place the groats into a bowl of water for 2 hours to saturate and puff.
2. Strain the groats and mix with all the other ingredients.

SHRIMP SALAD
garidosalata

Serves: 6-8

Preparation time: 30'   Cooking time: 8'   Degree of difficulty: ❶△△   Nutritional value: △❶△
Taste: ❶△△   Calories: 516

1 small, chopped lettuce
4-6 leaves salad lettuce
1 kg. (2.2 lb.) boiled
and cleaned shrimps
1 dose mayonnaise as described
in the recipe PINK MAYONNAISE
3 s.s. chopped parsley
salt and pepper

Preparation

1. Keep the heads on some of the shrimps to use as garnish.
2. Place one salad lettuce leaf into individual bowls.
3. Mix the chopped lettuce with the shrimps and the mayonnaise and fill the bowls.
4. Garnish with the parsley and the shrimps you kept aside.

PASTA & RICE

zimarika ke rizi

SPAGHETTI WITH SEAFOOD
spageti me thalasina

Serves: 4-6

Preparation time: 30' Cooking time: 30' Degree of difficulty: △❍△ Nutritional value: △❍△
Taste: △❍△ Calories: 639

  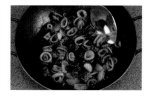

Preparation

500 gr. (1.1 lb.) spaghetti
5 small squids (calamari), finely chopped
300 gr. (10.6 oz.) small shrimps, cleaned
½ kg. (1.1 lb.) clams with their shell
½ kg. (1.1 lb.) mussels with their shell
cups cubed, peeled and seedless tomatoes
2 cloves garlic, finely chopped
3 s.s. finely chopped parsley
2 t.s. hot paprika / ½ cup dry white wine
t.s. sugar / 4 s.s. olive oil / salt and pepper

1. Clean and wash the clams and the mussels and boil in a pot with a little water. Place the covered pot on the fire and leave for 10' until the seafood shells opens.

2. Strain the seafood and keep their broth. Keep a few in their shell and clean the remainder.

3. Sauté the garlic in oil together with the squid, add 3-4 s.s. broth and boil for 5'. Add all the remaining ingredients(except for the spaghetti) and allow the sauce to boil on a low fire for 15'.

4. In the meantime, boil the spaghetti in salted water, add the broth from the seafood and strain.

5. Place the spaghetti onto a platter and pour the seafood sauce on top. Sprinkle finely chopped parsley on top and serve immediately.

SPAGHETTI WITH LOBSTER
astakomakaronada

Serves: 4
Preparation time: 10'   Cooking time: 30'   Degree of difficulty: △⊙△   Nutritional value: △⊙△
Taste: △⊙△   Calories: 592

Preparation

500 gr. (1.1 lb.) spaghetti
1 lobster about 1 kg. (2.2 lb.)
or 4 small lobsters about 250 gr.
(8.8 oz.) each or crawfish
2 cups cubed, peeled and
seedless tomatoes
2 cloves garlic
3 s.s. parsley, finely chopped
½ cup dry white wine
4 s.s. olive oil / salt and pepper

1. Scald the lobster in salted water that has been boiling for 5' and strain, keeping the broth.
2. Sauté the garlic in olive oil and add the lobster cut into two, lengthwise. Turn the lobster a little inside the pot and add the wine, tomatoes and parsley. Boil for 10'.
3. In the meantime, boil the spaghetti in salted water, add the broth from the lobster and strain.
4. Place the spaghetti onto a platter and pour the lobster sauce on top. Scatter finely chopped parsley on top and serve immediately.

KNOTS WITH TUNA
fiongakia me tono

Serves: 4
Preparation time: 25'   Cooking time: 20'   Degree of difficulty: ⊙△△   Nutritional value: △⊙△
Taste: △⊙△   Calories: 687

Preparation

500 gr. (1.1 lb.)
fiongakia paste
2 cups tinned tuna that has
been strained
and cut into pieces
Tomato sauce, as described in the
recipe "SPAGHETTI NAPOLITAN"
2 s.s. capers / 10 olives / salt

1. Boil the spaghetti in plenty of salted water, in accordance with the manufacturer's instructions.
2. Prepare the tomato sauce, remove it from the fire and add the capers, olives and tuna
3. Strain the spaghetti, place it on a platter and pour the sauce over it.
4. Serve the fiongakia immediately.

MANESTRA WITH VEAL
giouvetsi me moshari

Serves: 6-8

Preparation time: 15'   Cooking time: 2 hours   Degree of difficulty: ❍△△   Nutritional value: △△❍
Taste: △❍△   Calories: 747

Preparation

1 kg. (2.2 lb.) veal
with a little fat, cut into pieces
2 cups tomato puree
2 cups sliced, peeled,
seedless tomatoes 1 onion,
finely chopped
½ t.s. sugar
500 gr. (1.1 lb.)
barley-shaped pasta (kritharaki)
2 t.s. butter
½ cup olive oil / salt and pepper

1. Sauté the onion and the meat with olive oil, add 1 cup hot water and boil the food on a low fire for 1 hour.

2. Put the raw kritharaki into a ceramic or baking dish with a lid and add the meat, oil, tomatoes, sugar, salt, pepper and a little water.

3. Bake with the food covered at 180°C for about 30', remove the lid and cook for another 20' until it has cooked and little sauce has remained. Add a little boiling water during the cooking stage, if necessary.

MEAT WITH SPAGHETTI - A CORFIATE DISH
pastitsada kerkyraiki

Serves: 6-8

Preparation time: 15'   Cooking time: 2 hours   Degree of difficulty: ⚫△△   Nutritional value: △△⚫

Taste: △⚫△   Calories: 738

1 kg. veal cut into pieces
1 onion, grated
2 cups tomato puree
1 s.s. tomato puree diluted in
½ cup hot water.
½ cup red wine
3-4 clove spikes
1 cinnamon stick
½ cup olive oil
500 gr. thick spaghetti
4 s.s. butter
1 cup grated Corfu
or Kefalotiri cheese
salt and pepper

Preparation

1. Sauté the onion with the olive oil, add the meat and sauté together. Add a little water, the wine, cloves and cinnamon and boil the food on a low fire for 1 hour.

2. Add the tomato, salt and pepper and boil the food for about 30', until the meat becomes tender and remains in its sauce.

3. Boil the spaghetti in plenty of salted water and strain. Put the butter into a pan and scorch it , then pour it over the spaghetti.

4. Serve the meat with the spaghetti sprinkled with the grated cheese.

SHELL-SHAPED SPAGHETTI WITH FRESH TOMATOES & FETA
kohilia me freskia domata ke feta

Serves: 4

Preparation time: 15′   Cooking time: 20′   Degree of difficulty: ◐△△   Nutritional value: △◐△
Taste: ◐△△   Calories: 588

Preparation

500 gr. (1.1 lb.)
shell-type spaghetti
2 cups grated feta cheese
2 cups tomatoes cut into
cubes, peeled and
without seeds
5 s.s. basil
4 s.s. olive oil
salt and pepper

1. Boil the spaghetti in plenty of salted water, in accordance with the manufacturer's instructions.
2. Mix the tomatoes with the basil
3. Strain the spaghetti, place on a platter and douse with the raw oil.
4. Cover with the tomato and basil, followed by the cheese.
5. Sprinkle a little freshly grounded pepper and serve immediately.

LINGUINI WITH BROCCOLI & FETA
linguini me brokolo ke feta

Serves: 8

Preparation time: 10′   Cooking time: 20′   Degree of difficulty: ◐△△   Nutritional value: △◐△
Taste: ◐△△   Calories: 503

Preparation

1 kg. (2.2 lb.) linguini
1 small broccoli
cut into bunches
2 garlic cloves, finely chopped
4 spring onions,
finely chopped
1½ t.s. thyme
2 cups feta cheese
8 t.s. grated parmesan cheese
8 s.s. olive oil
salt and pepper

1. Cook the broccoli in steam for 5′ until it softens a little.
2. Sauté the spring onions (shallots) and the garlic with the olive oil and add the thyme and broccoli. Sauté together for 2′-3′.
3. Boil the spaghetti in plenty of salted water, in accordance with the manufacturer's instructions.
4. Strain the spaghetti, place onto a platter and sprinkle with the broccoli and feta.
5. Serve the linguini immediately, sprinkled with the parmesan.

OCTOPUS WITH MACARONI

chtapodi me kofta makaronakia

Serves: 4-6

Preparation time: 15'   Cooking time: 45'   Degree of difficulty: ❶△△   Nutritional value: △❶△
Taste: △❶△   Calories: 614

800 gr. (1,8 lb.) octopus
500 gr. (1.1 lb.)
small macaroni
1 onion, grated
1 cup tomato puree
1 s.s. tomato paste
diluted in ½ cup hot water.
2 bay leaves
3 s.s. parsley, finely chopped
5 s.s. olive oil
salt and pepper

Preparation

1. Boil the octopus in a little water for 30' or until it is tender. Strain and keep the water.

2. Sauté the onion with the olive oil, add the octopus cut into pieces and turn it around and stir to sauté for a few minutes. Add the remaining ingredients and 2 cups of the strained water (in which the octopus was cooked), and cook the food on a medium fire for 10'-15' until all the water has evaporated. Add a little water if needed.

3. Serve the food hot or cold, sprinkled with parsley.

PASTICCIO
pastitsio

Serves: 12

Preparation time: 50'   Cooking time: 45' - 50'   Degree of difficulty: △◑△   Nutritional value: △△◑
Taste: △△◑ · Calories: 512 το κομμάτι

Preparation

500 gr. (1.1 lb.)
macaroni for pasticcio,
or pennes or rigatoni
1 cup grated kefalograviera
cheese
2 s.s. melted butter
mincemeat and cream as
in the recipe for "MOUSAKA"

1. Boil the macaroni in salted water, strain and pour the hot melted butter over it, which has previously been "burnt" on the fire.
2. Allow the macaroni to cool for a while and then mix with the cheese.
3. Put half the macaroni into a long, narrow baking dish, then place a layer of mincemeat on top, followed by a layer of the remaining macaroni.
4. Put the cream on top of the macaroni, as for "MOUSAKA", and bake at 180°C for about 45'-50' or until the surface has browned.

RAVIOLI WITH CHALOUMI
Homemade Pasta from the Cypriat Cuisine
ravioles me chaloumi

Serves: 4-6

Preparation time: 40'   Cooking time: 15'   Degree of difficulty: △△◐   Nutritional value: △△◐
Taste: △◐△   Calories: 748

Preparation

For the dough:
½ kg. (1.1 lb.) flour
150-200 ml. cold water
2 eggs lightly beaten
½ t.s. salt
For the filling:
200 gr. (7 oz.) grated
chaloumi cheese
2 eggs
1-2 t.s. dry mint,
finely copped
For the garnishing:
75 gr. (2.6 oz.) melted
butter or olive oil
100 gr. (3.5 oz.) grated
chaloumi cheese

1. Sift the flour, make a hole in the middle and add the salt and eggs. Mix the ingredients and slowly add the water. Knead well until a soft dough is formed.

2. For the filling, mix the eggs, cheese and mint in a bowl

3. Roll out the dough into a thin sheet about 3 mm thick and cut into disk shapes with a glass or a coup-pat.

4. Put a spoonful of filling onto each dough disk, wet the edges with a little water and fold in half to form half-moon shapes. Press the edges well to stick together, thus keeping the filling inside.

5. Boil the ravioli a little at a time in plenty of salted water or chicken or meat broth for about 10'-15'.

6. Remove the ravioli with a skimmer and place onto a platter, pour on top the butter or hot oil, sprinkle with the cheese and serve immediately.

Alternative: You can also fill the ravioli with mincemeat. In order to prepare the mincemeat, follow the recipe for "KOUPES"

RICE WITH PRAWNS

rizi me garides

Serves: 4-6

Preparation time: 40'   Cooking time: 25'   Degree of difficulty: ❶△△   Nutritional value: △❶△
Taste: △❶△   Calories: 635

Preparation

2 cups rice
tomato sauce, as described
in the recipe "SPAGHETTI
NAPOLITAN"
1 pepper cut into pieces
1 kg. (2.2 lb.) prawns
1 t.s. Tabasco sauce

1. Scald the prawns in water that has been boiling for 5', then sauté them and keep the broth. Clean the prawns and keep a few with their heads for garnishing.
2. Prepare the tomato sauce, replacing the basil with 2 s.s. finely chopped parsley finely chopped and add the pepper and the Tabasco sauce. Add the prawns just before the sauce is ready.
3. Boil the rice with 5 cups of the broth from the prawns (if it is not enough, supplement with water).
4. Serve the rice with the prawn sauce poured over it.

RISOTTO MARINARA

rizoto marinara

Serves: 6-8

Preparation time: 30'   Cooking time: 20'   Degree of difficulty: ❶△△   Nutritional value: △❶△
Taste: △❶△   Calories: 530

½ kg. (1.1 lb.) small prawns
and crawfish, cleaned
½ kg. (1.1 lb.) very small
squid (calamari)
½ kg. (1.1 lb.) various
sea-foods (mussels, oysters, pines,
barnacles, etc.), cleaned.
2 onions, finely chopped
2 garlic cloves
2 cubed, peeled, seedless tomatoes
2 cups rice / ½ cup dry white wine
3 s.s. parsley, finely chopped
1 t.s. sweet or hot paprika
½ cup olive oil / salt and pepper

Preparation

1. Sauté the onion and garlic with the olive oil and when brown, add the rice and mix in the pot to sauté for a few minutes. Add the seafood, prawns and squid and mix the food so as to sauté all the food.
2. Add the tomatoes, wine, paprika, salt, pepper and 4-5 cups water.
3. Boil the food on a medium fire for 20' and add the parsley 5' before the food is removed from the fire.

Spaghetti with Garlic & Parmesan

spageti me skordo ke parmezana

Serves: 4

Preparation time: 25′   Cooking time: 20′   Degree of difficulty: ❍△△   Nutritional value: △❍△

Taste: △❍△   Calories: 520

Preparation

500 gr. (1.1 lb.)
spaghetti
2 garlic cloves, sliced
6 s.s. parmesan cheese,
coarsely grated
6 s.s. olive oil
salt

1. Boil the spaghetti in plenty of salted water, in accordance with the manufacturer's instructions.
2. Put the oil in a pan to scorch and add the garlic. When the garlic browns, add the parmesan and allow it to brown a little.
3. Strain the spaghetti, place in a bowl and add the oil with the garlic and parmesan.
4. Serve the spaghetti immediately, sprinkling it with the grated parmesan.

Note: You add very little salt to the spaghetti as it is boiling, because it will become very salty when the parmesan cheese is added.

Clams with Fresh Oregano, Aromatic Wild Greens & Parmesan

achivadakia me freskia rigani, aromatika horta ke parmezana

Serves: 4

Preparation time: 5′   Cooking time: 20′   Degree of difficulty: ❍△△   Nutritional value: △❍△

Taste: △❍△   Calories: 512

Preparation

500 gr. (1.1 lb.)
salted clams
2 s.s. fresh
oregano,
finely chopped
1 s.s. basil, finely chopped
1 t.s. thyme
1 t.s. dry oregano
1 t.s. rosemary
6 s.s. parmesan
salt

1. Boil the spaghetti in plenty of salted water, in accordance with the manufacturer's instructions.
2. Put the oil in a pan to scorch and add the dry oregano, thyme and rosemary.
3. Strain the spaghetti, place in a bowl and add the oil with the spices
4. Add the remaining fresh ingredients to the spaghetti, mix well, sprinkle on the parmesan and serve the clams immediately.

RICE WITH SQUID
rizi me kalamarakia

Serves: 4-6

Preparation time: 20'   Cooking time: 20'   Degree of difficulty: ❍△△   Nutritional value: △❍△

Taste: △❍△   Calories: 680

Preparation

1 kg. (2.2 lb.) squid
(calamari)
1½ cups rice
1 onion, finely chopped
3 cups tomato puree
tomato paste
s.s. parsley, finely chopped
red pepper, finely chopped
1 t.s. Tabasco sauce
½ cup dry white wine
1/3 cup olive oil
salt and pepper

1. Clean and wash the squid and throw away the thin bone, the eyes and the entrails.

2. Put in a pot with ½ cup water and allow them to boil a while in their own broth.

3. When the squid absorbs all the liquid, add the oil and onion and allow to sauté.

4. Add all the remaining ingredients and cook the food for about 20'-25', until the squid and the food remains in its own sauce.

RISOTTO WITH AROMATIC WILD GREENS
rizoto me aromatika chorta

Serves: 4-6

Preparation time: 20'   Cooking time: 20'   Degree of difficulty: ❍△△   Nutritional value: ❍△△
Taste: ❍△△   Calories: 600

Preparation

2 cups rice
½ cup spring onions (shallots),
finely chopped
1 s.s. parsley, finely chopped
1 s.s. anise, finely chopped
1 s.s. estragon, finely chopped
½ cup dry white wine
½ cup grated parmesan
or pekorino cheese
6 s.s. olive oil
salt and pepper

1. Sauté the spring onions (shallots) with the olive oil, add the rice and sauté for a few minutes.
2. Add 5 cups hot water and the remaining ingredients and allow the rice to boil on a low fire for 20'-25' until the liquid evaporates.
3. Serve the risotto hot, sprinkled with cheese.

RISOTTO WITH MUSHROOMS
rizoto me manitaria

Serves: 4-6

Preparation time: 20'   Cooking time: 20'   Degree of difficulty: ❍△△   Nutritional value: △❍△
Taste: ❍△△   Calories: 620

Preparation

2 cups rice
½ cup spring onions (shallots),
finely chopped
500 gr. (1.1 lb.)
chopped mushrooms
cut into pieces
1 s.s. parsley, finely chopped
½ cup dry white wine
1 s.s. anise, finely chopped
½ cup grated parmesan or
pekorino cheese
6 s.s. olive oil
salt and pepper

1. Sauté the spring onions with the olive oil, add the rice and sauté for a few minutes.
2. Add the mushrooms, sauté them together with the rice and when they brown a little, add 5 cups hot water and the remaining ingredients and allow the rice to boil on a low fire for 20'-25' until the liquid evaporates.
3. Serve the risotto hot, sprinkled with cheese.

MEALS IN OIL & LENTEN FOOD
ladera ke nistisima

Peas with Corn Cooked in Oil

arakas me kalampoki laderos

Serves: 6-8

Preparation time: 10'   Cooking time: 40'   Degree of difficulty: ❍△△   Nutritional value: △❍△
Taste: ❍△△   Calories: 400

Preparation

1 kg. (2.2 lb.) peas
½ kg. (1.1 lb.) corn
2 carrots
6-7 chopped shallots
5 s.s. chopped anise
1 s.s. tomato paste diluted
in ½ cup warm water
½ cup olive oil
salt and pepper

1. Sauté the shallots with the oil, until brown.
2. Add the peas, the corn, the carrots and 1 cup water and cook the casserole on medium heat for 15'-20'.
3. Add the tomato paste, the anise, salt and pepper and if needed, a little more water.
4. Allow the casserole to cook for 15'-20' more, or until the liquid evaporate.

OKRA IN OIL
bamies laderes

Serves: 6-8

Preparation time: 30'   Cooking time: 40'   Degree of difficulty: ❶△△   Nutritional value: ❶△△

Taste: △❶△   Calories: 425

Preparation

1 kg. (2.2 lb.) okra
1 chopped onion
2 cups cubed tomatoes
2 sliced tomatoes
1 t.s. tomato paste diluted
in ½ cup warm water
6 s.s. chopped parsley
2/3 cup olive oil
salt, pepper
and ½ t.s. sugar

1. Cut the top part of the okra, where the stem is. Salt them, sprinkle with vinegar, place on a pan and place in the sun for approximately 1 hour until they dry out and the sticky liquid in their interior disappears. Wash the okra and place in a strainer to strain.

2. Sauté the onion in half of the olive oil, add the tomato cubes, the tomato paste, salt, pepper and sugar and simmer the sauce for approximately 10'.

3. Scald the okra in boiling water for 5', strain them and place them in a fire resistant pan.

4. Spread out the tomato slices over the okra and pour the remaining olive oil over the food.

5. Broil at 180° C for approximately 30', or until the liquids evaporate, leaving the dish in its sauce. During cooking, you shouldn't stir the food because the okra will mash and they won't keep their shape.

Note: You can cook the okra in a pot instead of boiling them, simmering for approximately 15' so they won't mash.

LENTILS WITH RICE
From the Cypriat Cuisine
moutzerta

Serves: 6-8

Preparation time: 10'   Cooking time: 50'-60'   Degree of difficulty: ❶△△   Nutritional value: △△❶

Taste: △❶△   Calories: 586

Preparation

½ kg. (1.1 lb.) large lentils
½ cup rice
2 sliced onions
6 s.s. olive oil
salt and pepper

1. Cook the lentils in plenty of water and when they are half-cooked, add the rice.

2. Cook the dish on a low heat for approximately 20', or until the liquids evaporate.

3. Sauté the onions in olive oil, add to the dish and serve warm.

STUFFED TOMATOES
domates gemistes

Serves: 6

Preparation time: 45'   Cooking time: 1½ hours   Degree of difficulty: △ ◐ △   Nutritional value: △ ◐ △
Taste: △ ◐ △   Calories: 695

Preparation

8 large tomatoes
4 peppers
12 zucchini flowers (optional)
2 grated zucchinis
5-6 sliced potatoes
2 cups rice
2 grated onions
2 crushed garlic cloves
5-6 s.s. chopped parsley
2 s.s. chopped mint
½ cup dark raisins (optional)
½ cup pinecone (optional)
1 cup olive oil
salt, 2 t.s. sugar and pepper

1. Cut a slice from the top of each tomato and empty its contents with a spoon. Beat the tomato interiors that you removed in the blender, so as to make a paste.
2. Salt the tomato paste and sprinkle with a little sugar.
3. Cut the top part of each pepper and clear out the seeds.
4. Sauté the onion and the garlic in half the oil and when they're lightly brown, add the zucchini and then the rice and stir in the pot so as to sauté lightly. Add 2/3 of the tomato paste, salt and pepper and lower the heat to simmer for 5'.
5. Remove the rice from the heat and add the parsley, the mint, the raisins and the pinecone.
6. With this mixture stuff the tomatoes, the peppers and the zucchini flowers, place the slices you removed earlier on top and place on a pan, adding the potatoes. Salt and pepper and pour the remaining tomato paste and the oil over them.
7. Broil at 180° C for approximately 1½ hours, or until the vegetables turn brown, adding a little water if necessary.

Note: You should not stuff the vegetables to the top, because the rice will rise when cooked. The grated zucchini makes the filling juicier.

Artichoke, Carrot & Potato Casserole

aginares a la polita

Serves: 8

Preparation time: 40'   Cooking time: 40'   Degree of difficulty: △△⊙   Nutritional value: ⊙△△
Taste: ⊙△△   Calories: 430

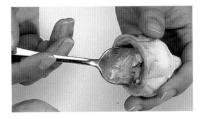

Preparation

8 artichokes
4-5 chopped shallots
4 carrots in round slices
4 sliced potatoes
5 s.s. chopped anise
2/3 cup olive oil
salt and pepper

1. Clean the artichokes, removing the stalks, the tough leaves and the fuzz from their interiors and rub with lemon juice so that they won't turn dark.
2. Put the cleaned artichokes into a bowl of water covering them, in which you will have diluted 1 tablespoon flour.
3. Sauté the shallots in the oil and add the artichokes with the water in the bowl and the remaining ingredients.
4. Allow the casserole to cook for approximately 40', or until all the liquids evaporate and the artichokes are tender. If necessary, add a little more water.

Broiled Artichokes in Aromatic Olive Oil

aginares psites me aromatiko eleolado

Serves: 8

Preparation time: 10'   Cooking time: 40'   Degree of difficulty: ⊙△△   Nutritional value: ⊙△△
Taste: ⊙△△   Calories: 250

Preparation

8 artichokes
salt and pepper
½ cup aromatic olive oil

1. Cut the stalks from the artichokes.
2. Without any more cleaning, rub them with aromatic olive oil and place in a pan.
3. Broil at 180°C for approximately 40'.
4. The artichokes are consumed as such: cut the leaves one by one with your hands and holding it by its pointy end, dip into a bowl of aromatic olive oil and eat its tender part. When only the heart of the artichoke remains, remove the fuzz with a teaspoon and dip in olive oil before eating it.

Aromatic olive oil: beat 8 tablespoons olive oil in a bowl, 3 tablespoons lemon juice, 2 tablespoons mustard, 1 crushed garlic clove, 1 tablespoon chopped parsley, salt and pepper.

EGGPLANTS STUFFED WITH CHEESE

melitzanes papoutsakia me tiri

Serves: 8-10

Preparation time: 50'   Cooking time: 40' - 45'   Degree of difficulty: △❍△   Nutritional value: △△❍
Taste: △△❍   Calories: 593

Preparation

1 kg. (2.2 lb.) oblong eggplants (5 medium size eggplants)
300 gr. (10.6 oz.) kefalograviera cheese
3 eggs
3 s.s. chopped parsley
5 s.s. olive oil, plus as much as necessary for frying
10 t.s. melted butter
5 s.s. grated toast
béchamel sauce, as described in the recipe MOUSAKAS

1. Cut the eggplants lengthwise down the middle and sprinkle with salt. Allow them to stand for ½ hour and then wash in plenty of water, so that the bitterness goes away and squeeze them in your hands to strain them.

2. With a teaspoon empty out part of each eggplant interior and lightly fry the emptied eggplants in oil. Place them on absorbent paper towels to strain the oil.

3. Chop the insides of the eggplants. Sauté the onion and the insides of the eggplants in 6 tablespoons oil. Remove from the heat and after allowing to cool, add the cheese, the eggs and the parsley.

4. Fill the emptied out eggplants with this mixture and cover the top with a crème such as the one described in the MOUSAKAS recipe.

5. Dab 1 teaspoon melted butter on each stuffed eggplant, sprinkle with the grated toast and broil at 180° C for approximately 40'-45', or until their surface browns.

Note: select eggplants with a nice shape and of similar size so that the dish will have a nice appearance.

Variation: if you want to stuff the eggplants with mincemeat, replace the cheese and eggs with the mincemeat, as described in the MOUSAKAS recipe.

EGGPLANT FROM IKARIA

soufiko ikarias

Serves: 6

Preparation time: 30'   Cooking time: 30'   Degree of difficulty: ❍△△   Nutritional value: △❍△
Taste: △❍△   Calories: 475

1kg. (2.2lb) eggplants
2 cups cubed, peeled, seedless tomatoes
1 chopped onion
3 chopped garlic cloves
3 s.s. chopped parsley / 1 t.s. sugar
250 gr. (8.8 oz.) grated feta cheese
flour to cover the eggplants
6 s.s. olive oil
and as mush as necessary for frying
salt and pepper

Preparation

1. Cut the eggplants into thick slices and sprinkle with salt. Leave them in a bowl with the salt for about ½ hour and then wash them with plenty of water, so that the bitterness will go away and squeeze them in your hands to strain them.

2. Flour the eggplants and fry them in hot oil.

3. Sauté the onion and the garlic in the oil and add the tomatoes, the sugar and the pepper, boiling the sauce for 5'. You needn't add salt because the food will be salty due to the feta cheese.

4. Place the eggplants in a pan, cover them with the sauce and sprinkle with the parsley and the feta cheese.

5. Broil at 180° C for approximately 30' to 40' and serve either hot or cold.

EGGPLANT, ZUCCHINI & POTATO CASSEROLE
briam

Serves: 6-8

Preparation time: 30'   Cooking time: 60'   Degree of difficulty: ❍△△   Nutritional value: △❍△

Taste: △❍△   Calories: 482

Preparation

½ kg. (1.1 lb.) round sliced eggplants
½ kg. (1.1 lb.) round sliced zucchini
½ kg. (1.1 lb.) diced potatoes
1 diced pepper
2 sliced onions
2-3 sliced garlic cloves
2 cups cubed tomatoes
1 s.s. tomato paste diluted in ½ cup warm water
6 s.s. chopped parsley
1 cup olive oil
salt, pepper and ½ t.s. sugar

1. Sprinkle the eggplants with salt, let them stand for approximately 1 hour and then wash them with plenty of water so that the bitterness will go away and squeeze them in your hands to strain them.

2. Place all the ingredients in a pan, cover them with aluminium foil and broil at 180° C for approximately ½ hour.

3. Remove the aluminium foil and broil for ½ hour more, or until the vegetables are tender and the liquids evaporate. If necessary, add a little water.

GARBANZO BEANS CASSEROLE
revithia sifneika

Serves: 6-8

Preparation time: 20'   Cooking time: 1½ ώρα   Degree of difficulty: ❍△△   Nutritional value: △△❍

Taste: △❍△   Calories: 477

Preparation

½ kg. (1.1 lb.) peeled
garbanzo beans
1 s.s. soda
1 s.s. tomato paste diluted
in ½ cup warm water
2 grated onions
2 bay leaves
1 twig rosemary
2/3 cup olive oil
salt and pepper

1. Put the garbanzo beans in a bowl of water with the soda for at least 12 hours.

2. Wash them with plenty of water, strain them and place them in a pot of water covering them, along with the remaining ingredients.

3. Cook them for approximately 45' and then place them in a clay pot with a cover, or in a fire resistant pot with a cover, if you don't have a clay one.

4. Place them in the oven and cook at a low heat for another 45' at 150°C, or until the garbanzo beans are tender and the liquids evaporate. If necessary, add a little more warm water.

STUFFED EGGPLANTS
melitzanes imam

Serves: 4

Preparation time: 45'   Cooking time: 60'   Degree of difficulty: △❂△   Nutritional value: △❂△

Taste: △△❂   Calories: 495

Preparation

8 long eggplants, from Argos preferably
4 sliced large onions
3 sliced garlic cloves
2 cups cubed tomatoes
1 s.s. tomato paste diluted in ½ cup warm water
8 s.s. chopped parsley
4 s.s. olive oil and as much as necessary for frying
salt, pepper and paprika

1. Cut the stems from the eggplants and carve two-three sides lengthwise.

2. Sprinkle with salt and let them stand for approximately 1 hour. Wash them with plenty of water, so that the bitterness goes away, and squeeze them in your hands to strain them. Fry the eggplants in olive oil until they are lightly brown.

3. Boil the onions in a little water and a little salt until they are tender and all the water evaporates.

4. Mix the onions with the garlic, the tomato and the tomato paste, the paprika, the salt and the pepper and fill the openings you carved in the eggplants with this mixture.

5. Place the eggplants in a pan, sprinkle with the parsley and pour the oil over the dish.

6. Broil at 180°C for approximately 1 hour, or until the liquids evaporate, leaving the dish in its sauce.

FRIED ZUCCHINI & EGGPLANT
kolokithia ke melitzanes tiganita

Serves: 6-8

Preparation time: 40'   Cooking time: 30'   Degree of difficulty: ❂△△   Nutritional value: ❂△△

Taste: ❂△△   Calories: 324

Preparation

300 gr. (10.6 oz.) zucchini
300 gr. (10.6 oz.) eggplants
mash for frying (as described in the recipe FRIED TOMATOES)
olive oil for frying
salt and pepper

1. Cut the eggplants and the zucchini in thin slices and sprinkle with salt.

2. Place the zucchini slices on a towel to absorb their juices.

3. Leave the eggplants in the salt for about ½ hour and then rinse with plenty of water, so the bitterness will go away and squeeze them in your hands to strain.

4. Dip the eggplants and the zucchini in the mash and fry in hot oil.

5. Serve with tzatziki or yoghurt dip.

ROASTED GIANT BEANS IN SAUCE
gigantes plaki

Serves: 6-8

Preparation time: 15'   Cooking time: 60'   Degree of difficulty: ⚫△△   Nutritional value: △△⚫

Taste: △△⚫   Calories: 486

Preparation

½ kg. (1.1 lb.) giant beans
2 grated onions
4 finely chopped garlic cloves
2 cups tomato puree
5 s.s. chopped parsley
1 t.s. sweet paprika
1 t.s. hot paprika
(depending on your tastes)
½ t.s. sugar
2 bay leaves
2/3 cup olive oil
salt and pepper

1. Place the beans in a basin with water for at least 12 hours.
2. Boil them until they are tender and then strain them.
3. Sauté the onion and the garlic in the oil, add the remaining ingredients and simmer the sauce for 5'.
4. Place the beans in a fire resistant pan, pour the sauce over them and broil at 180°C for approximately an hour, or until the liquids evaporate.

FRIED PEPPERS
piperies tiganites

Serves: 6

Preparation time: 10'   Cooking time: 15'   Degree of difficulty: ❶△△   Nutritional value: ❶△△

Taste: △△❶   Calories: 160

Preparation

½ kg. (1.1 lb.) long,
green peppers
3 s.s. vinegar
olive oil for frying
salt and pepper

1. Wash and dry the peppers.
2. Puncture them in several places with a fork, dry again
(so that they won't splatter during frying) and fry in hot oil.
3. Place them in a small platter, salt and pepper them and pour the
vinegar over them.
4. Serve with tzatziki or yoghurt dip.

RICE WITH SPINACH & LEEKS
rizi me spanaki ke prasa

Serves: 6

Preparation time: 30′ Cooking time: 30′ Degree of difficulty: ❶△△ Nutritional value: △❶△
Taste: △❶△ Calories: 406

Preparation

1 kg. (2.2 lb.) spinach
½ kg. (1.1 lb.)
chopped leeks
½ cup rice
1 chopped onion
5 s.s. chopped anise
1 s.s. tomato paste
diluted in ½ cup of water
3/4 cup olive oil
salt and pepper

1. Clean the spinach, wash it and chop it. Place it in a pot with boiling salted water, boil for 5′ and strain it.
2. Boil the leeks with a little water and salt, until they are tender and all the water evaporates.
3. Pour the oil in the pot with the leeks, add the onion and sauté for a few minutes, until they are lightly brown.
4. Add the spinach, stir it so as to lightly sauté it and allow it to absorb the liquids, then add the rice.
5. Stir the rice also to lightly sauté it and then add the diluted tomato paste, 2 cups boiling water, anise, salt and pepper.
6. Simmer for approximately 30′ or until the liquids evaporate and the food remains only with the oil. If the rice hasn't cooked enough yet, add some more water.

LEEKS & ARTICHOKES IN A TOMATO SAUCE
prasa ke aginares kokinista

Serves: 8

Preparation time: 40′ Cooking time: 40′ Degree of difficulty: △△❶ Nutritional value: ❶△△
Taste: △❶△ Calories: 325

Preparation

8 artichokes
1 kg. (2.2 lb.) chopped leeks
5 s.s. chopped anise
1 cup tomato juice
1 s.s. tomato paste diluted in
½ cup warm water
2 lemons
2/3 cup olive oil
salt and pepper

1. Clean the artichokes, removing the stalks, the tough leaves and the fuzz from their interior and rub them with lemon juice so that they won't turn dark.
2. Boil the leeks with a little water and a little salt until they are tender and all the water evaporates.
3. Pour the oil in the pot with the leeks and sauté for a few minutes, until lightly brown.
4. Add the artichokes and 1 cup hot water and allow the casserole to cook on medium heat for 15′-20′.
5. Add the tomato juice and paste, anise, salt and pepper and, if needed, a little more water.
6. Allow the casserole to cook for 15′-20′ more, or until the liquids evaporate and the artichokes are tender.

CABBAGE & RICE ROLLS

lachanodolmades me rizi

Serves: 6
Preparation time: 60'   Cooking time: 40'   Degree of difficulty: △△⊙   Nutritional value: ⊙△△
Taste: △⊙△   Calories: 463

1 medium sized red
or green cabbage,
approximately 1 kg. (2.2 lb.)
4-5 s.s. vinegar
1½ cup rice
2 grated onions / 4 s.s. anise
1 grated sour apple
½ cup dark raisins
½ cup pinecone
2/3 cup olive oil
salt and pepper

Preparation

1. Place the cabbage in a pot of boiling water in which you've added half the vinegar and salt. When the cabbage is tender and its leaves start to separate, you remove it with a skimmer and separate the leaves.

2. Sauté with half the oil and the onion, adding the rice and stirring to lightly sauté. Add ½ cup boiling water and simmer for a few minutes, until all the liquids evaporate.

3. Remove the rice from the heat and add the anise, the sour apple, the raisins, the pinecone, salt and pepper.

4. With the rice mixture and the cabbage leaves you make rolls. Place some cabbage leaves on the bottom of a pot and place the cabbage and rice rolls in a circular manner and in layers.

5. Add hot water, enough to cover the cabbage and rice rolls, the remaining oil and vinegar, salt and pepper and cover with a dish, so that while boiling, the cabbage and rice rolls will remain in place.

6. Cook the casserole for approximately 40' on medium heat until all the water is evaporated, try it and if the rice isn't well cooked yet add a little more water.

Eggplant Pie

mousakas

Serves: 10

Preparation time: 60'   Cooking time: 40'-45'   Degree of difficulty: △△◐   Nutritional value: △△◐
Taste: △△◐   Calories: 920

Preparation

For the base:
1½ kg. (3,3 lb.) sliced
eggplants
½ kg. (1.1 lb.) sliced potatoes
olive oil for frying
salt and pepper
For the filling:
½ kg. (1.1 lb.) mincemeat
2 grated onions
2 crushed garlic cloves
2 cups tomato juice
3 egg whites
4-5 s.s. grated toast
6 s.s. grated kefalograviera
cheese
1 bay leaf
1 cinnamon stick
1 t.s. paprika
3-4 s.s. chopped parsley
4-5 s.s. olive oil
salt and pepper
For the covering:
3 cups milk
9 s.s. flour
9 s.s. butter
5-6 pieces fresh butter
3 egg yolks
1/3 t.s. grated nutmeg
salt and pepper

1. Cut the eggplants into thin slices and sprinkle with salt. Let them stand with the salt for approximately ½ hour and then wash with plenty of water, so the bitterness will go away and squeeze them in your hands to strain them.

2. Fry them in hot oil and place them on absorbent paper towels to strain from the extra oil. Fry the potatoes, salt them and place them in an oblong fire resistant pan, so as to cover its bottom. Lay out half of the eggplants on top.

3. Sauté the onion in the oil, add the garlic and the mincemeat and sauté for a few minutes, until the mincemeat browns. Add the tomato, the laurel, the cinnamon, the paprika, the salt and pepper and cook until the liquids evaporate.

4. When the mincemeat cools, remove the bay leaf and the cinnamon stick, add the parsley, half the grated toast, the egg whites and the cheese and lay them out on top of the eggplants. Lay out the remaining eggplants over the mincemeat.

5. Sauté the flour in the butter for about 5' and when it browns, remove from the heat and add all the milk, after warming it. Stir the mixture quickly with a whisk and place on the heat source. Continue stirring over low heat until the cream sets.

6. Remove from the heat and add the salt, the pepper and the nutmeg and when it cools add the egg yolks. Pour the cream over the mousaka, distribute the fresh butter pieces over it and sprinkle with the remaining grated toast.

Bake at 180° C for approximately 40'-45', or until the surface turns brown.

FISH & SEAFOOD
psaria ke thalasina

SEA BREAM IN TOMATO SAUCE
sinagrida a la spetsiota

Serves: 6-8
Preparation time: 15'   Cooking time: 60'   Degree of difficulty: ❍△△   Nutritional value: △❍△
Taste: △❍△   Calories: 500

Preparation

1½ kg. (3,3 lb.) sea bream,
or other large fish, in slices
3 cups strained tomatoes
2 crushed garlic cloves
5 s.s. chopped parsley
1 cup grated toast
½ cup dry, white wine
2/3 cup olive oil
salt and pepper

1. Coat the fish slices with a little oil and sprinkle with salt and pepper. Place the slices in a pan.
2. Mix the tomatoes, the garlic, the parsley, the wine, the oil, the salt and pepper in a bowl, and pour some of this mixture onto the fish.
3. Sprinkle a little grated toast and pour a little tomato sauce on the fish once again.
4. Repeat this procedure, finishing with the grated toast, so that there is a grated toast, parsley and sauce coating on the fish, which will turn into a crust when broiled.
5. Broil at 180° C for approximately 1 hour, splashing the coated fish slices with their sauce every so often.

FLOUNDER FILETS IN TOMATO & OLIVE SAUCE
fileta glossas me sauce domatas ke elies

Serves: 6
Preparation time: 10'   Cooking time: 20'   Degree of difficulty: ❍△△   Nutritional value: △❍△
Taste: ❍△△   Calories: 420

Preparation

6 large flounder filets
2 cups tomato juice
1 grated small onion
1 chopped garlic clove
1 t.s. oregano
10 chopped black olives
6 s.s. olive oil
salt and pepper

1. Coat the flounder filets with a little oil and sprinkle with the oregano, salt and pepper. Broil them in a pan at 200° C for approximately 20'.
2. With the remaining oil sauté the onion and the garlic, add the tomato and cook at a medium heat until the sauce sets. Add the olives to the sauce 5' before it's ready.
3. Serve the broiled filets along with the sauce and garnish with a few roasted onion rings.

SHRIMP STEW WITH TSIKOUDIA
garides giouvetsaki me tsikoudia

Serves: 4-6

Preparation time: 30'   Cooking time: 30'-40'   Degree of difficulty: ❂△△   Nutritional value: △△❂
Taste: △△❂   Calories: 617

Preparation

1 kg. (2.2 lb.) shrimp
1 onion cut in pieces
1 carrot
1 celery stalk
1 bay leaf
1 t.s. granulated pepper
2 sliced garlic cloves
3 s.s. tsikoudia
3 cups cubed, peeled,
seedless tomatoes
4 s.s. chopped parsley
1 t.s. paprika
pepper
250 gr. (8.8 oz.)
6 s.s. olive oil

1. Scald the shrimp for 3'-4' in a little boiling water, clean them and keep some of the heads for garnishing.
2. Boil the heads in the same water in which you boiled the shrimp, together with the onion, the carrot, the celery, the bay leaf and the granulated pepper, so that a cup of broth remains after you strain it.
3. Sauté the garlic in the oil, add the shrimp and sauté for a few minutes. Add the tsikoudia and light it with a match. Douse with the shrimp broth
4. Place the shrimp in individual clay pots or in a fire resistant pan and pour the tomato, the parsley and the feta on them. Sprinkle with the paprika and the pepper and garnish with the shrimp heads you kept aside. Do not add salt to the dish, as the feta cheese is salty.
5. Broil at 200° C for 30', or until the surface of the dish browns.

GARLIC FRIED SHRIMP
garides skordates

Serves: 4-6

Preparation time: 40'   Cooking time: 10'   Degree of difficulty: ❂△△   Nutritional value: △❂△
Taste: △△❂   Calories: 450

Preparation

1 kg. (2.2 lb.) shrimp
2 chopped garlic
cloves
4 s.s. parsley
8 s.s. olive oil
salt and pepper

1. Clean the shrimp and keep some of the heads.
2. Sauté the garlic and the shrimp in the oil for a few minutes, until they brown and the juices evaporate.
3. Sprinkle with the parsley, salt and pepper and serve immediately.

BOUILLABAISSE
psarosoupa kakavia

Serves: 6-8
Preparation time: 40'   Cooking time: 40'   Degree of difficulty: △❍△   Nutritional value: △△❍
Taste: △❍△   Calories: 456

Preparation

1½ kg. (3,3 lb.) various large
and small fish (blackfish,
gre fish, sea scorpion, grouper)
½ kg. (1.1 lb.) various seafood:
mussels, shrimp, crawfish,
lobster, crab (optional)
2 potatoes cut in 4
2 onions cut in 4
2 cups cubed, peeled
and seedless tomatoes
1 garlic clove
1 bay leaf
1 twig thyme
3 s.s. chopped parsley
1 cup dry white wine
½ t.s. saffron
1 cup sea water (optional)
the juice of 1 lemon
½ cup olive oil
salt and pepper

1. Place the onions, the garlic, the tomato, the bay leaf and the thyme into a pot and boil them with a little water for 30'. Add the potatoes and then the cleaned fish over them.
2. Pour in the seawater, the wine and as much water as necessary so as to cover the fish, and lastly, the olive oil. Add the saffron, the pepper and salt (if you are using seawater, add the salt at the end of cooking, after trying the soup, so that it's not too salty) and boil the soup for approximately 15'-20'.
3. Serve the soup warm, with lemon juice, sprinkled with the parsley. Serve the various fish on a platter, or ration together with the soup.

Note: The bouillabaisse must be made with very fresh fish, especially rockfish, like the ones mentioned in the ingredients. Because these fish have a lot of bones, if they are very small and can't be eaten, boil them alone first for 30', strain them by pressing them in the strainer, so their broth comes out. Then add the remaining ingredients and the larger fish, if any, to this broth and continue with the recipe as described above.

MARINADED RED MULLET
barbounia marinata

Serves: 6-8
Preparation time: 40'   Cooking time: 40'   Degree of difficulty: △○△   Nutritional value: △△○
Taste: △○△   Calories: 675

Preparation

1½ kg. (3,3 lb.) red mullet
2 chopped garlic cloves
2 cups tomato juice
½ cup vinegar
3-4 s.s. chopped parsley
1 t.s. rosemary
1 t.s. thyme
1 bay leaf
1 t.s. sugar
1 cup olive oil + more for frying
4 s.s. flour, and as much
as necessary to flour the fish
before frying
salt and pepper

1. Clean the fish, sprinkle with salt and flour them. Fry them in hot oil and arrange in a platter.

2. Strain the oil from the fried residue, (you should have 1 cup of oil; if it is less, add some more raw oil), place it in a fryer and add the flour.

3. Stir the flour to sauté it until it browns. Add 2 glasses of water and the vinegar and stir, so as to have a smooth mixture. Add the tomato, the garlic, the sugar, the rosemary, the thyme, the bay leaf, the salt and pepper and cook at medium heat for 15'-20'. Strain the sauce and pour it over the fish before serving.

Note: In older times, when refrigerators didn't exist, this manner of cooking also constituted a food preservation technique, preserving the food for a few days. For this reason the quantity of the vinegar was double to what we use here, and the sauce completely covered the fish.

SEAFOOD PIES

vol-o-van me thalassina

Serves: 8

Preparation time: 15′   Cooking time: 30′   Degree of difficulty: ❍△△   Nutritional value: △△❍

Taste: △❍△   Calories: 472

8 individual pie shells
200 gr. (7 oz.) smoked, tinned and strained clams
200 gr. (7 oz.) small shrimp, cooked and cleaned
400 gr. (14 oz.) tinned asparagus, cut into pieces
1 chopped onion
4 s.s. flour
12 s.s. asparagus juice
300 gr. (10.5 oz.) cream
1 s.s. chopped anise
1 s.s. chopped parsley
4 s.s. olive oil
salt and pepper

Preparation

1. Sauté the onion in the oil, sprinkle in the flour and stir until light brown.
2. Add the asparagus juice and the cream, while stirring continuously.
3. Simmer for 4′-5′ and add all the remaining ingredients.
4. Bake the empty pie shells for approximately 30′, until they brown and fluff. Fill the pie shells with the seafood mix and serve immediately, while they're still warm.

MUSSELS PILLAF
mydia pilafi

Serves: 4

Preparation time: 15'   Cooking time: 20'   Degree of difficulty: ❶△△   Nutritional value: △❶△
Taste: △❶△   Calories: 470

Preparation

0 gr. (1,3 lb.) cleaned mussels
1 chopped onion
½ cup dry white wine
3 s.s. chopped parsley
1 pepper cut in rings
½ cup olive oil
1 cup rice
1 fish bouillon cube
salt and pepper

1. Boil the rice with 2½ cups of water and 1 fish bouillon cube.
2. A little before the rice is cooked, add the mussels, already cooked in accordance with the "MUSSELS CASSEROLE" recipe.

COD IN TOMATO SAUCE
bakaliaros plaki

Serves: 4-6

Preparation time: 30'   Cooking time: 60'   Degree of difficulty: △○△   Nutritional value: △△○

Taste: △○△   Calories: 605

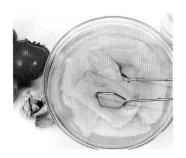  

Preparation

1 kg. (2.2 lb.) cod, or bass filets
4 sliced onions
3 sliced garlic cloves
3 cups tomato puree
1 s.s. tomato paste,
diluted in ½ cup warm water
4 s.s. chopped parsley
4 medium size potatoes,
cut in round slices
½ cup olive oil
salt and pepper

1. If you use salted cod, skin it, remove the bones and cut it into pieces. Place the cod pieces into a bowl of water for approximately 15 hours, changing the water 3-4 times, so that the fish will de-salt.

2. Oil a pan, place the potatoes in it and sprinkle with salt and pepper (if you are using salted cod, be careful with the salt so that the dish won't be too salty).

3. Place the pieces of the fish on the potatoes.

4. Boil the onions in a little water until they are tender and the water evaporates. Add the oil and sauté for a few minutes. Add the garlic and the tomatoes and pour this sauce over the fish and potatoes.

5. Sprinkle with the parsley, the salt and pepper and broil at 180° C for approximately 1 hour.

SWORDFISH KEBAB
xifias souvlaki

Serves: 6 (12 kebabs)
Preparation time: 20'   Cooking time: 7'-8'   Degree of difficulty: ❂△△   Nutritional value: △❂△
Taste: ❂△△   Calories: 460

Preparation

1 kg. (2.2 lb.) swordfish
cut in cubes
2 onions in square pieces
2 peppers in square pieces
15 baby tomatoes cut in half
1 s.s. oregano
2 s.s. lemon juice
6 s.s. olive oil
salt and pepper
12 kebab skewers

1. Whisk the lemon juice, the olive oil, the oregano, the salt and pepper in a bowl, place the swordfish pieces into it and place it in the refrigerator for approximately 1 hour.
2. Skewer the swordfish pieces, with onion, pepper and tomato pieces between the fish pieces.
3. Coat the kebabs with the remaining oil mixture and barbecue or grill them on both sides, for a total of 7'-8'.

OCTOPUS IN WINE SAUCE
chtapodi krasato

Serves: 4-6

Preparation time: 20'   Cooking time: 30'   Degree of difficulty: ❍△△   Nutritional value: △❍△
Taste: △△❍   Calories: 570

Preparation

1 kg. (2.2 lb.) cooked octopus cut in pieces
4-5 sliced onions
4 whole garlic cloves
1 cup tomato juice
1 s.s. tomato paste diluted in ½ cup warm water
1 glass dry red wine
2 bay leaves
1 s.s. seasoning
1 t.s. granulated pepper
1 t.s. sweet or hot paprika
1 cinnamon stick
½ cup olive oil / salt and pepper

1. Boil the onions in a little water until they are tender and all the water evaporates. Add the oil and sauté for a few minutes, until they brown.
2. Add the garlic and the octopus and stir in the oil. Then add all the remaining ingredients.
3. Cook for approximately 30', until the octopus is tender and the sauce sets.

Note: Add the salt just before removing the stew from the fire and after trying it, as sometimes the octopus is too salty.

Variation: Octopus and onion stew is cooked in the same way, but you must replace half of the onions with ½ kg. (1.1 lb.) baby onions which you must fry and add to the stew approximately 15' before it is ready. Also add a twig of rosemary.

Broiled Sardines in Tomato Sauce
sardeles me domata sto fourno

Serves: 6

Preparation time: 20'   Cooking time: 45'   Degree of difficulty: ❂△△   Nutritional value: △△❂
Taste: △❂△   Calories: 426

Preparation

1 kg. (2.2 lb.) sardines
5 sliced garlic cloves
2 cups cubed, peeled,
seedless tomatoes
1 s.s. oregano
½ cup olive oil
salt and pepper

1. Wash and clean the fish, removing the head and bone, if you like.
2. Place the fish in a pan, sprinkle with salt and pour the tomato, garlic and oil over them.
3. Sprinkle with salt, pepper and oregano and broil at 180°C for approximately 45'.

Broiled Trout
pestrofa sto fourno

Serves: 4

Preparation time: 15'   Cooking time: 20'   Degree of difficulty: ❂△△   Nutritional value: △❂△
Taste: △❂△   Calories: 450

Preparation

4 trout
1 lemon
1 cup fresh bread crumbs
1 chopped garlic clove
3 s.s. chopped parsley
½ cup dry white wine
4 s.s. olive oil
salt and pepper

1. Clean the fish, cut the lemon in two and rub it on the trout, inside and out. Add salt and pepper. Squeeze the lemon and keep the juice that's left over.
2. Heat the oil in a pan, remove from the fire and place the crumbs in it, the garlic and the parsley. Spread half of the mixture in a pan and place the fish on it.
3. Sprinkle the fish with the remaining mixture and the lemon juice.
4. Broil in a preheated oven at 180°C for 5' and add the wine. Continue broiling for approximately 10'-15' more, until the fish browns, splashing it with its juices every so often.

SEAFOOD CREPES
krepes me thalassina

Serves: 6

Preparation time: 45'-60'   Cooking time: 30'   Degree of difficulty: △△❍   Nutritional value: △△❍
Taste: △❍△   Calories: 425

For the crepes:
1 cup flour
1 cup and 4 s.s. milk
2 eggs
2 s.s. melted butter or margarine
+ more if needed for frying
salt
For the filling:
1 cup cleaned and boiled shrimp
1 cup cleaned and boiled clams
cup boiled lobster or crab meat
2 s.s. chopped shallots
2 s.s. chopped parsley
½ cup dry white wine
1 t.s. flour
6 s.s. olive oil
salt and pepper

Preparation

1. Stir all the ingredients for the crepes together in a bowl using a whisk, and fry them one by one in a non-stir frying pan, in a little butter.
2. Sauté the onions in the olive oil and then add the seafood and sauté until brown.
3. Add the wine, the flour, the salt and pepper and simmer for a few minutes, until the sauce sets. Sprinkle with the parsley.
4. Fill the crepes with the seafood mixture and serve immediately.

COD CROQUETTES
kroketes bakaliarou

Serves: 4-6

Preparation time: 30'   Cooking time: 10'   Degree of difficulty: △△❍   Nutritional value: △❍△
Taste: △❍△   Calories: 687

Preparation

1 kg. (2.2 lb.) boiled cod
cut in pieces
1 cup boiled, mashed potatoes
1 cup béchamel
2 eggs
4 s.s. chopped parsley
flour and olive oil for frying
salt, pepper
and a little grated nutmeg

1. Mix the mashed potatoes with the béchamel, and when they cool add the eggs and the cod pieces, so that they're dough-like.
2. Place the mixture in the refrigerator to harden for 2-3 hours, and then mould into balls.
3. Flour the balls made out of the mixture and fry them in hot oil. Sprinkle with the parsley and serve them warm. Accompany with garlic sauce (skordalia) (see recipe).
For the béchamel: Sauté 3 s.s. flour with 3 s.s. butter for approximately 5' and when it browns remove from the fire and add 1 cup warm milk.
Stir the mixture quickly using a whisk, and place on the fire again. Add salt, pepper and nutmeg and continue stirring on a low heat, until the cream sets.

Squid with Anise & Green Olives

soupies me anitho ke prasines elies

Serves: 4-6

Preparation time: 30'   Cooking time: 40'-45'   Degree of difficulty: △❂△   Nutritional value: △❂△

Taste: △❂△   Calories: 465

1 kg. (2.2 lb.) squid
1 chopped onion
6-7 chopped shallots
6-7 s.s. chopped anise
6-7 s.s. fennel
4 s.s. chopped parsley
1 cup green olives
½ cup dry white wine
6 s.s. olive oil
salt and pepper

Preparation

1. Clean and wash the squid and discard the bone, the eyes, the ink and the entrails.

2. Place them in a pot without adding water, so that they cook in their own juices.

3. When the juices evaporate, add the oil and the onions and allow them to sauté. Add the wine, the salt and pepper and simmer for approximately 30'.

4. Add all the remaining ingredients and cook for approximately 10'-15' more, until the squid is tender and the sauce sets.

Variation: Squid with spinach is cooked in the same way, but you must replace the olives with 1 kg. (2.2 lb.) chopped, fresh spinach or 700 gr. (1,9 lb.) frozen spinach, eliminate the funnel and, if you like, add ½ cup black raisins.

Note: You can pour some of the squid ink along with the wine into the casserole, so as to give it a distinctive, dark colour.

Mussels Casserole
mydia saganaki

Serves: 6

Preparation time: 10'   Cooking time: 10'   Degree of difficulty: ❍△△   Nutritional value: △❍△
Taste: △❍△   Calories: 357

Preparation

1 kg. (2.2 lb.) mussels
1 chopped onion
½ cup dry white wine
3 s.s. chopped parsley
1 pepper cut in rings
½ cup olive oil
salt and pepper

1. Wash and rub the musselshells well, until the fuzz disappears. Rinse them and place them on absorbent paper towels to dry. Add the mussels, the wine, the salt and pepper and cook for a few minutes.
2. Sprinkle with parsley and serve.

BROILED SEA BASS
lavraki sto fourno

Serves: 6

Preparation time: 15′ Cooking time: 40′ Degree of difficulty: ❍△△ Nutritional value: △❍△

Taste: ❍△△ Calories: 485

Preparation

1½ kg. (3,3 lb.) sea bass
or other large fish
1 cup dry white wine
2 s.s. lemon juice
3 t.s. mustard
½ cup olive oil
salt and pepper

1. Clean and wash the fish, sprinkle with salt and place it in a pan.
2. Beat the mustard, the lemon, the wine, the oil and the salt and pepper and pour it over the fish.
3. Broil at 180° C for approximately 40′, splashing it with the sauce every so often.

GROUPER FLAMBE WITH OUZO
sfirida flampe me ouzo

Serves: 6

Preparation time: 10′ Cooking time: 20′ Degree of difficulty: ❍△△ Nutritional value: △❍△

Taste: △❍△ Calories: 386

Preparation

6 grouper slices
2 crushed garlic cloves
3 s.s. chopped parsley
2 s.s. lemon juice
1 shot ouzo
6 s.s. olive oil
salt and pepper

1. Coat the fish slices with olive oil and sprinkle with the salt, pepper, garlic and parsley.
2. Barbecue or grill the fish for approximately 20′.
3. Place the fish slices on a metal platter, pour the ouzo over them (after warming them a little), light with a match and douse with the lemon juice

Note: Light the ouzo at the time you are bringing the platter to the table to serve, so that you offer a spectacular show to your dinner guests.

STUFFED CALAMARI

kalamarakia gemista

Serves: 4-6

Preparation time: 40'   Cooking time: 30'   Degree of difficulty: △△◐   Nutritional value: △◐△
Taste: △◐△   Calories: 550

Preparation

1 kg. (2.2 lb.) medium size calamari
2/3 cup rice
2 grated onions
1 chopped garlic clove
3 s.s. chopped parsley
1 chopped red pepper
1 cup tomato juice
1 s.s. tomato paste diluted
in ½ cup warm water
½ dry white wine
½ t.s. sugar
1 t.s. sweet or hot paprika
1 s.s. raisins and 1 s.s. pinecones
(optional)
½ cup olive oil
salt and pepper

1. Clean and wash the calamari, removing the head and flippers and discarding the bone and entrails. Chop the head and flippers.
2. Sauté 1 onion, the garlic, the pepper and the chopped heads and flippers in half of the olive oil, until they brown and the liquids evaporate. Add the rice and the tomato paste, salt and pepper and simmer for 3'-4'.
3. Add the parsley, the paprika, the raisins and the pinecones and stuff the calamari. Use a toothpick to close up the opening on each calamari, so the stuffing won't come out.
4. Sauté the other onion in the rest of the olive oil and add the tomato juice, the wine, the sugar, salt and pepper.
5. Arrange the stuffed calamari in a pot, add the tomato sauce and cook on medium fire for approximately 30', until they are tender and the sauce sets. If needed, add a little water during cooking.

MEAT & POULTRY

kreas ke poulerika

FRICASSEE LAMB
arnaki frikase

Serves: 8-10

Preparation time: 40'   Cooking time: 1½-2 hours   Degree of difficulty: △○△   Nutritional value: △○△
Taste: ○△△   Calories: 607

Preparation

2 kg. (4,4 lb.) lamb
cut into pieces
1 kg. (2.2 lb.) chopped shallots
1 kg. (2.2 lb.) lettuce
or endives cut in pieces
6 s.s. chopped anise
2/3 cup olive oil
salt and pepper
For the egg and lemon sauce:
2 eggs
½ cup lemon juice
1 t.s. flour

1. Scald the shallots in boiling water for 5' and strain.
2. Sauté the lamb pieces until brown, add 1 cup boiling water and simmer for approximately 90', or until it's almost tender.
3. Add the shallots, the anise and the greens, the salt and pepper and continue cooking for approximately 30', until there is only a little broth.
4. Beat the eggs and slowly add the lemon juice, in which you have diluted the flour. At the end of cooking, remove the food from the fire and pour the egg and lemon sauce over it, quickly moving the pot in a circular motion to distribute the sauce evenly. Serve immediately.

VEAL & ZUCCHINI CASSEROLE
moshari me kolokithakia

Serves: 6

Preparation time: 30'   Cooking time: 1 hour and 30'   Degree of difficulty: ❍△△   Nutritional value: △❍△

Taste: △❍△   Calories: 660

Preparation

1 kg. (2.2 lb.) veal cut in pieces
1 kg. (2.2 lb.) small zucchinis
1 grated onion
3 cups tomato juice
1 s.s. tomato paste, diluted
in ½ cup warm water
½ t.s. sugar
½ cup olive oil and more
for frying

1. Sauté the pieces of veal with the oil and when they brown, add the onion and let it brown.
2. Add 1 cup boiling water to the veal and let it simmer on a low heat. If needed, add a little more water.
3. Clean the zucchini and fry in hot olive oil, until brown.
4. When the veal is tender and the liquids have evaporated, add the tomato, the tomato paste, the sugar, salt and pepper and boil for 5'.
5. Add the zucchinis and cook the food for approximately 10'-15', or until the liquids evaporate and only the sauce remains.

Variation: It is customary for egg and lemon sauce to be poured on this dish. Even though it is a rule that dishes which contain tomatoes are not served with egg and lemon sauce, this variation is especially tasty and worth trying. Beat 2 eggs and little by little add ½ cup lemon juice, in which you have diluted 1 teaspoon flour. At the end of cooking, pull the food from the heat and immediately pour the egg and lemon juice over it, quickly moving the pot in a circular motion to evenly distribute the sauce. Serve immediately.

CHICKEN IN LEMON SAUCE
kotopoulo me sauce apo lemoni

Serves: 6

Preparation time: 10'   Cooking time: 50'   Degree of difficulty: ❍△△   Nutritional value: △❍△

Taste: ❍△△   Calories: 445

Preparation

6 portions chicken,
breasts or legs
juice and gratings
from ½ lemon
2 s.s. flour
4 s.s. olive oil
salt and pepper

1. Sauté the chicken in the oil in a deep pan, and when it browns, add ½ cup water, the lemon gratings, salt and pepper.
2. Simmer the casserole for approximately 50' and when the chicken is tender in the oil, remove it with a skimmer.
3. Add flour to the broth which remained in the pan and sauté until it browns. Add the lemon juice and 1 cup water and simmer the sauce for 2'-3', so that the sauce sets and is neither too thick nor too thin.
4. Pour the sauce over the chicken and serve with mashed potatoes or rice.

VEAL WITH OLIVES
moshari me elies

Serves: 6

Preparation time: 10'   Cooking time: 2 hours   Degree of difficulty: ❍△△   Nutritional value: △❍△

Taste: △❍△   Calories: 616

1 kg. (2.2 lb.) veal cut in pieces
15 small onions,
whole and cleaned
2 chopped garlic cloves
1 cup tomato puree
1 s.s. tomato paste diluted
in 1 cup warm water
½ t.s. thyme
1 cup meat broth
1 cup pitted olives
4 s.s. chopped parsley
½ cup olive oil
flour to cover the pieces of meat
salt and pepper

Preparation

1. Sprinkle the meat with salt and pepper and flour the pieces.
Sauté in oil, add the garlic and sauté for a few more minutes.
2. Add the broth, the tomato puree and paste and the thyme and place
the food into a clay pot with a cover or in a fire resistant pot.
3. Roast at 180°C for 90' and add the olives, the sautéed onions and the
parsley.
4. Roast for another 30', until the meat is tender in its sauce.

STUFFED LAMB
arni gemisto

Serves: 12-14
Preparation time: 45'   Cooking time: 3 hours   Degree of difficulty: △○△   Nutritional value: △△○
Taste: △△○   Calories: 795

Preparation

1 lamb breast,
approximately 3 kg. (6,6 lb.)
1 lamb pluck
1 cup rice
½ kg. (1.1 lb.) chopped shallots
5 s.s. chopped parsley
5 s.s. chopped anise
3 s.s. chopped mint
1 egg
2 t.s. cinnamon
1 t.s. cumin
1 t.s. seasoning
1 cup tomato puree
1 s.s. tomato paste diluted
in 1 cup warm water
2/3 cup olive oil
salt and pepper

1. Wash the lamb breast and sprinkle with salt and pepper inside
and out.
2. Scald the lamb pluck in boiling water for 5' and chop.
3. Sauté in half of the oil and the onions and add the lamb pluck pieces
and then the rice. Stir them all together, remove from the heat and after it
cools add the egg, the parsley, the anise, the mint, the seasoning, salt and
pepper.
4. Stuff the lamb breast and fasten with toothpicks so that the stuffing
won't come out.
5. Put the lamb breast in a pan and pour the tomato and the remaining
oil over it.
6. Cover the lamb with aluminium foil and roast at 180° C for
approximately 2 hours and then remove the aluminium and roast for
1 more hour, until the lamb is crispy.

Note: If you wish you can remove the bones before stuffing. You can also
add ½ cup raisins, ½ cup pinecones or ½ cup peeled almonds to the
stuffing. If the lamb pluck is small, add some mincemeat.

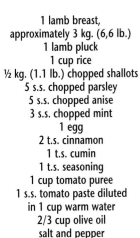

FILETS IN GREEN PEPPER
fileto me prasino piperi

Serves: 6

Preparation time: 10'   Cooking time: 10'   Degree of difficulty: ⭕△△   Nutritional value: ⭕△△
Taste: △△⭕   Calories: 470

Preparation

6 veal filets
2 s.s. green pepper
3 s.s. tsikoudia
6 s.s. tomato paste
3 t.s. flour
3 s.s. chopped parsley
3 s.s. chopped shallots
6 s.s. olive oil
salt

1. Place a heavy non-stick pan on the fire and sprinkle with salt when it's hot. When the salt begins to brown, add the filets and cook for 30". Turn them on the other side, reduce the cooking fire a little and continue to cook for as long as necessary, depending on how well done you want the filets.
2. Place the filets onto a platter (taking care so that they're kept warm) and pour the remaining oil in the pan. Sauté the onions with the pepper and then add the flour. Stir quickly and when the flour browns, add ½ cup of water and stir again, so that you get a smooth mixture.
3. Add the tsikoudia to the sauce, the tomato and a little salt and let it simmer for 5'-10', until it's firm.
4. Pour the sauce over the filets, sprinkle with the parsley and serve immediately.

PORTERHOUSE STEAK WITH ROASTED TOMATOES
psaronefri me psites domates

Serves: 6

Preparation time: 15'-20'   Cooking time: 15'-30'   Degree of difficulty: ⭕△△   Nutritional value: △⭕△
Taste: △⭕△   Calories: 456

Preparation

3 porterhouse steaks
(pork filets)
of approximately 350 gr.
(12.3 oz.) each
4 tomatoes in round slices
6 s.s. olive oil
3 t.s. oregano
salt and pepper

1. Cut each steak lengthwise in the middle and pound with the special utensil.
2. Coat them with olive oil, sprinkle with salt and pepper and grill them until they brown on both sides.
3. Place the round tomato slices on the steaks, pour the remaining oil over them and sprinkle with salt, pepper and oregano.
4. Grill once more, until the tomatoes are grilled and brown.

Variation: You can barbecue the porterhouse steaks instead of grilling. In this case you will barbecue the tomatoes separately, and then place them on the steaks to serve.

VEAL & PORK MEATBALLS WRAPPED IN SHEEP SKINS
From the Cypriat Cuisine
seftalies

Serves: 8-10
Preparation time: 60'   Cooking time: 20'   Degree of difficulty: △△◐   Nutritional value: △◐△
Taste: △△◐   Calories: 630

½ kg. (1.1 lb.) veal mince
½ kg. (1.1 lb.) pork mince
2-3 grated onions
6 s.s. chopped parsley
2 s.s. grated toast
2 s.s. grated mint
1 t.s. cinnamon
2 s.s. olive oil
1 sheep skin (bolia)
salt and pepper

Preparation

1. Wash the sheep skin in plenty of cold water and a little vinegar and place in a warm place until it softens.
2. Mix the mincemeat with the other ingredients and knead well. If the mixture is hard, add 2-3 tablespoons water. Place the mincemeat mixture in the refrigerator for 1 hour.
3. Spread the sheep skin and cut into square pieces of approximately 12 X 12 cm. Place 1 tablespoon mincemeat mixture on each bolia piece and roll to make little "packages".
4. Place the seftalies for a few hours in the refrigerator to set, then skewer them on wooden skewers and barbecue or grill them for approximately 20', until they brown and are well cooked. You can also roast them in the oven.
5. Serve them warm, with lemon, chopped parsley and onion.

Meat Cooked in a Clay Pot
kreas sti gastra

Serves: 8-10

Preparation time: 15'   Cooking time: 3 hours   Degree of difficulty: ⚙△△   Nutritional value: △⚙△
Taste: △△⚙   Calories: 556

Preparation

1 kg. (2.2 lb.) veal pieces
½ kg. (1.1 lb.) lamb pieces
00 gr. (0,44 lb.) hard kefalotyri
cheese or pecorino cheese
2-3 crushed garlic cloves
1 s.s. oregano
½ cup olive oil
pepper

1. Wash the meat, dry with absorbent paper towels and place in the clay pot.
2. Add the garlic, the oregano, the olive oil and the pepper, cover the pot and place in the oven. Cook at 170°C for 2 hours, without preheating the oven.
3. Uncover the clay pot and add the cubed cheeses in walnut size cubes. If needed, add some boiling water. Don't add salt because the cheeses are salty enough.
4. Increase the temperature to 200°C and cook for 1 more hour, or until the meat is tender and brown.

Note: If the pot you will use is made of clay, it must be placed in a cold oven, otherwise it will crack. If you don't own a clay pot you can use a metal one or a fire resistant pot with a cover.

MINCEMEAT ROLL WITH AROMATIC GREENS STUFFING

rolo me kima ke gemisi apo aromatika chorta

Serves: 8

Preparation time: 15'   Cooking time: 1 hour and 30'   Degree of difficulty: ❍△△   Nutritional value: △△❍
Taste: △❍△   Calories: 472

Preparation

½ kg. (1.1 lb.) veal mince
½ kg. (1.1 lb.) pork mince
1 grated onion
2 eggs
4 s.s. grated toast
5 strips of bacon
8 s.s. olive oil
salt and pepper
For the filling:
4 eggs
250 gr. (8.8 oz.) grated
mozzarella or emental cheese
4 s.s. chopped parsley
2 s.s. dry, grated estragon
1 s.s. dry thyme
1 s.s. oregano

1. Knead all the ingredients well with 3 tablespoons of the oil, leaving out the bacon.
2. Spread the mincemeat mixture out on a grease wrapping paper sheet sized 30 x 15 cm., so that the dimensions of the mixture are about the same as those of the paper sheet.
3. Beat the eggs and fry the omelette in hot oil. Place the omelette on the mincemeat, so that you cover about 3/4 of its surface, and sprinkle with the cheese and condiments.
4. Wrap the mincemeat mix in a roll, lifting the grease wrapping paper sheet a little so as to facilitate the wrapping process and place the mincemeat roll on an oblong, fire resistant pan.
5. Place the bacon slices on the roll, pour the remaining oil over it and roast at 180°C for approximately 90', or until the roll browns. If needed, add a little water to the roll.
6. To serve, cut the roll into slices, after allowing it to cook a little, and if you like you can accompany it with tomato sauce (see the recipe for SOUTZOUKAKIA sauce).

LAMB & VEGETABLES
From the Cypriat Cuisine
tavas

Serves: 6-8

Preparation time: 40'   Cooking time: 1½-2 hours Degree of difficulty: ❍△△   Nutritional value: △❍△
Taste: △❍△   Calories: 764

1 cubed lamb leg,
approximately 2 kg. (4.4 lb.)
½ kg. (1.1 lb.) potatoes
½ kg. (1.1 lb.) zucchini
4 onions
½ kg. (1.1 lb.) cubed, peeled,
seedless tomatoes
1 s.s. tomato paste diluted
in 1 cup warm water
s.s. grated cumin / 1 s.s. cinnamon
½ cup oil / salt and pepper

Preparation

1. Clean, wash and cut the vegetables into slices. Place in a clay pot with the pieces of lamb.
2. Add all the remaining ingredients, stirring and cooking at 180°C for approximately 1½ -2 hours. If needed, add some water during cooking.

PORK WITH PLUMS
chirino me damaskina

Serves: 8-10

Preparation time: 30'   Cooking time: 2 hours   Degree of difficulty: ❍△△   Nutritional value: △△❍
Taste: △❍△   Calories: 702

Preparation

2 kg. (2.2 lb.) boneless
pork leg
20 pitted plums
3 s.s. honey
3 s.s. mustard
2 s.s. lemon juice
2 t.s. ginger
2/3 cup olive oil
salt and pepper

1. Make lengthwise incisions in the pork leg, smear half of the olive oil or
it and sprinkle on salt and pepper.
2. Fill the incisions with the plums and tie the pork leg with cotton string.
3. Mix the remaining oil with the mustard, the honey, the lemon juice
and the ginger and smear it on the pork.
4. Roast at 180°C for approximately 2 hours, or until the pork is tender.
Let it cool, remove the string and cut into slices.
5. Serve with rice, roasted potatoes or mashed potatoes.

PORK WITH SOUR CABBAGE
chirino me xino lachano

Serves: 8-10

Preparation time: 30'   Cooking time: 2½ hours   Degree of difficulty: ❍△△   Nutritional value: △△❍
Taste: △❍△   Calories: 735

Preparation

2 kg. (2.2 lb.) pork cut in pieces
2 kg. (2.2 lb.) chopped, sour,
pickled cabbage
2 cups dry, white wine
3 s.s. tomato paste, diluted
in 1 cup warm water
2 onions
2 garlic cloves
2 whole carrots
2 bay leaves
½ t.s. cumin and pepper
1 s.s. granulated pepper
2/3 cup olive oil

1. It is preferable that the meat pieces are from the back of the animal.
Cook the pork for approximately 1 hour, with the carrots and garlic.
2. Strain the cabbage and wash in plenty of water. Squeeze it in your
hands to strain.
3. Sauté the onion with the olive oil, until it browns. Add the cabbage
and sauté for a few minutes. Add 2 cups broth and the tomato paste and
remove the pot from the heat.
4. Place the food in a fire resistant pot and add the pork and all the
remaining ingredients.
5. Roast at 170°C for approximately 90', or until the pork is tender and
the food remains in its sauce.

Note: You can replace the pickled cabbage with fresh, chopped cabbage
which you have boiled for 10', adding 3 tablespoons vinegar.

SCHNITZEL WITH SAUCE FROM CORFU
sofrito kerkyraiko

Serves: 6

Preparation time: 10'   Cooking time: 45'   Degree of difficulty: ❍△△   Nutritional value: △❍△
Taste: △❍△   Calories: 495

Preparation

6 beef slices for schnitzel, approximately 120 gr. (4.2 oz.) each
5 chopped garlic cloves
6 s.s. chopped parsley
5 s.s. vinegar or dry white wine
8 s.s. olive oil
3 t.s. flour
salt and pepper

1. In a deep frying pan, sauté the oil with the veal and the garlic until brown, add ½ cup of water, salt and pepper.
2. Cook the food on low heat for approximately 50' and when the meat is tender, with no juices other than the oil, remove it with a skimmer.
3. Place the remaining broth and the flour into the frying pan and sauté until brown. Add the vinegar or wine, the parsley and a little water and simmer the sauce so that it gets firm, neither too thick nor too thin.
4. Pour the sauce over the meat and serve with mashed potatoes or rice.

TOSSED MEATBALLS & POTATOES
From the Cypriat Cuisine
keftedes ke patates antinaktes

Serves: 6

Preparation time: 30'   Cooking time: 1 hour and 30'   Degree of difficulty: ❂△△   Nutritional value: △❂△
Taste: △❂△   Calories: 660

For the meatballs:
250 gr. (8.8 oz.) veal mince
250 gr. (8.8 oz.) pork mince
100 gr. (3.5 oz.) grated and strained potatoes
100 gr. (3.5 oz.) soaked and squeezed bread
1 egg / 1 grated onion
1 crushed garlic clove
3 s.s. chopped parsley
1 t.s. cinnamon
2 s.s. olive oil
+ as much as needed for frying
flour for frying, salt and pepper
For the potatoes:
1 kg. (2.2 lb.) small potatoes
1 cup dry red wine
4 s.s. coriander
1/3 cup olive oil / salt and pepper

Preparation

1. Mix all the ingredients for the meatballs together in a bowl, adding a little water to make the mixture fluffy. Place the mincemeat in the refrigerator for approximately 1 hour.

2. Mould the mincemeat mix into oblong shaped meatballs, flour them and fry them in hot oil.

3. Peel and wash the potatoes. Dry them well and fry them in hot oil in a deep frying pan with a cover.

4. When the potatoes brown, sprinkle with the coriander, salt and pepper and douse with the wine.

5. Cover the pot and toss 2-3 times, so as to stir the potatoes well. Continue cooking for approximately 15'-20', repeating the tossing about every 5'.

6. Serve warm.

Note: The potatoes are called "antinaktes" due to the way they are cooked, being tossed in the pot so as to stir them: antinasso means to toss.

STUFFED TURKEY
galopoula gemisti

Serves: 10-12

Preparation time: 45'   Cooking time: 2½ -3 hours (or in accordance to the packaging instructions)
Degree of difficulty: △❂△   Nutritional value: △△❂   Taste: △❂△   Calories: 857

1 turkey, approximately 5 kg.
10-11 lb.), including the entrails
½ kg. (1.1 lb.) mincemeat
50 gr. (5.3 oz.) chopped bacon
½ cup rice / 1 grated onion
200 gr. (7 oz.) chopped, cooked chestnuts
½ cup raisins
½ cup pinecones
juice and gratings of 1 orange
45 s.s. lemon juice
1 cup chicken broth
3 s.s. cognac / 1 apple
½ cup olive oil
salt and pepper

Preparation

1. Scald the entrails for 5', strain and chop them.

2. Fry the bacon in half the oil, until its fat melts. Remove the bacon pieces from the oil and sauté the onion, the mincemeat and the entrails.

3. Add the rice, the bacon, the chestnuts, the raisins, the pinecones, the orange juice and gratings, the chicken broth, the cognac, the salt and pepper. Remove the mixture from the fire and allow it to cool a little.

4. Sprinkle the turkey with salt and pepper and stuff it with the mixture. Place a whole apple in the opening so that the stuffing won't come out, but also to add nice aroma to the roast.

5. Put the turkey into a pan and pour the lemon and oil over it. Roast in accordance to the packaging instructions, splashing it with its juices every so often.

FRIED MEATBALLS
keftedes

Serves: 4-6

Preparation time: 15'   Cooking time: 15'   Degree of difficulty: ❍△△   Nutritional value: △❍△

Taste: △△❍   Calories: 700

Preparation

½ kg. (1.1 lb.) veal mince
3 soaked and squeezed
bread slices
1 grated onion
3/4 cup carbonated water
1 egg
1 s.s. ouzo
3 s.s. chopped parsley
3 s.s. chopped mint
flour for frying
2 s.s. olive oil
as much as needed for frying
salt and pepper

1. Mix all the ingredients and knead well. Place the mixture in the refrigerator for approximately 1 hour.

2. Mould the mixture into balls, flour them and fry them in hot oil.

3. Serve with boiled greens and French fried potatoes.

Variation: Knead the mixture for the meatballs as described in the recipe, replacing the carbonated water with beer and omitting the ouzo and the mint. Mould small, round meatballs and sauté in 6 tablespoons oil, adding 1 cup beer and cooking on a low fire for 15'. A little before it is done, add 4 tablespoons yoghurt and 2 tablespoons chopped parsley.

FRIED HAMBURGERS IN TOMATO SAUCE
soutzoukakia

Serves: 6

Preparation time: 15′   Cooking time: 45′   Degree of difficulty: ❂△△   Nutritional value: △△❂
Taste: △△❂   Calories: 849

Preparation

½ kg. (1.1 lb.) mincemeat
1 grated onion
2 crushed garlic cloves
3 slices stale bread
1 egg
1 t.s. cumin
4 s.s. olive oil + extra for frying
salt and pepper
For the sauce:
1 grated onion
2 chopped garlic cloves
2 cups tomato juice
1 s.s. tomato paste diluted
in ½ warm water
1 t.s. sugar
1 bay leaf
1 cinnamon stick
2 t.s. paprika
½ cup red wine
½ cup olive oil

1. Soak the bread in a bowl of water and when it's soft remove the crust. Squeeze it in your hands to remove most of the water.
2. Knead the mincemeat with all the ingredients well, adding 2-3 tablespoons of water.
3. Mould the mixture into oblong hamburgers, coat with a little oil and place in the refrigerator for 2-3 hours. Fry the soutzoukakia in hot oil.
4. For the sauce, sauté the onion and the garlic with the oil until brown and douse with the wine. Add the remaining ingredients and simmer the sauce at low heat for 5′.
5. Place the soutzoukakia in the pot with the sauce, moving the pot in a quick, circular motion to distribute the sauce evenly and simmer for about another 15′.
6. Serve the soutzoukakia with rice, noodles, French fried potatoes or mashed potatoes.

SKEWERED MEAT
souvlakia

Serves: 12
Preparation time: 30'   Cooking time: 15'-20'   Degree of difficulty: △❍△   Nutritional value: △△❍
Taste: △△❍   Calories: 450

Preparation

1 kg. (2.2 lb.) veal, pork, lamb
or chicken, in bite size pieces
2 sliced onions
4 sliced tomatoes
4 s.s. chopped parsley
12 souvlaki pitas
½ cup olive oil
sweet and hot paprika
salt and pepper

1. Sprinkle the meat pieces with salt and pepper and place them in a bowl with a little oil. Stir them so that they are all coated with oil and leave in the refrigerator for a few hours.
2. Skewer the meat and grill or barbecue.
3. Coat the pitas with a little oil and brown them in a non-stick frying pan or on the barbecue, taking care that they don't get too crispy, as they won't bend when you roll them around the souvlakia.
4. Mix the onion with the parsley.
5. In each pita place the meat from one skewer, 2-3 tomato slices, 1 tablespoon of the onion and parsley mixture, and sprinkle with salt and paprika.
6. Wrap the souvlakia in grease wrapping paper and serve. Accompany the souvlakia with tzatziki, French fried potatoes, choriatiki salad and feta cheese.

Note: You can serve the souvlakia "open", placing pieces of pita in a platter, the souvlakia over them, garnished with the remaining ingredients.

HARE OR RABBIT ONION STEW
lagos i kouneli stifado

Serves: 6-8

Preparation time: 15'   Cooking time: 2 hours   Degree of difficulty: △△◑   Nutritional value: △◑△

Taste: △◑△   Calories: 581

1 rabbit or hare, approximately
1½ kg. (3.3 lb.) cut in pieces
2 kg. (4.4 lb.) baby onions,
fresh or frozen
2 chopped onions
4-5 whole garlic cloves
3 cups tomato juice
2 s.s. tomato paste, diluted
in 1 cup warm water
2 bay leaves
1 twig rosemary
1 s.s. granulated pepper
1 s.s. granulated seasoning
4 s.s. olive oil + more for frying
salt and pepper
For the marinade:
½ cup olive oil / 1 cup red wine
3 s.s. vinegar / 1 t.s. sugar

Preparation

1. Place the rabbit pieces in a bowl, after washing them well and rinsing them with vinegar, and pour the marinade over them. Cover the bowl and place in the refrigerator for 2 days. Remove the rabbit from the bowl and dry the pieces with absorbent paper towels.

2. Sauté the rabbit in the oil and when it browns, add the onion and garlic and sauté for a few more minutes, until they brown.

3. Add the marinade ingredients and simmer the stew for approximately 1 hour. If needed add a little boiling water.

4. Add the remaining ingredients, except for the baby onions, and continue cooking for approximately ½ hour.

5. Clean the onions and fry them in hot oil. Strain them and add them to the stew.

6. Dilute 2 teaspoons flour in 1 cup of water and pour it into the stew. Let it simmer for approximately ½ hour more, or until the rabbit is tender and the sauce sets.

ROASTED CHICKEN WITH CONDIMENTS & POTATOES

kotopoulo psito me aromatika chorta ke patates

Serves: 6

Preparation time: 15'   Cooking time: 1 hour and 30'   Degree of difficulty: ❍△△   Nutritional value: △❍△

Taste: △❍△   Calories: 772

Preparation

1 chicken, approximately
1-1½ kg. (2.2 – 3.3 lb.)
1½ kg. (3.3 lb.) potatoes
cut in pieces
3 s.s. lemon juice
2 whole garlic cloves
2 crushed garlic cloves
1 twig basil
1 twig rosemary
1 s.s. thyme / 1 s.s. oregano
½ cup olive oil
1 lemon rind / salt and pepper

1. Wash the chicken and sprinkle with salt and pepper.
2. Sprinkle the interior of the chicken with salt and pepper and stuff with the condiments, the lemon rind and the two garlic cloves.
3. Use 2-3 toothpicks to close the opening in the chicken, so that the stuffing won't come out, and place in a pan face down.
4. Add the potatoes in the pan, sprinkle with salt and pepper and pour the lemon juice and olive oil over the roast.
5. Roast for 1 hour at 180° C. Turn the chicken on its other side, face up, and roast for another 30', or until the chicken browns. Add some boiling water during roasting, if necessary.

LAMB WITH PILAF

arni me pilafi anatolitiko

Serves: 8-10

Preparation time: 30'   Cooking time: 1½-2 hours   Degree of difficulty: ❍△△   Nutritional value: △△❍

Taste: △△❍   Calories: 845

Preparation

2 kg. (4.4 lb.) lamb
2 cups rice
100 gr. (3.5 oz.) kataifi
noodles
½ cup dark raisins
½ cup sliced, peeled almonds
1 chopped onion
2 mashed garlic cloves
1 t.s. each cinnamon, cumin,
hot paprika or sweet paprika
½ t.s. powdered cloves
2/3 cup olive oil
salt and pepper

1. Wash the lamb, sprinkle with salt and pepper and place it in a pan, without cutting it.
2. Mix half of the oil (keeping 1 tablespoon aside) with the garlic, the cinnamon, the cumin, the paprika and the cloves and sprinkle over the lamb.
3. Sauté the onion with the remaining oil and when it browns, add the rice and the almonds and sauté them with the onion for a few minutes. Add 5 cups boiling water, salt and pepper and let the rice simmer until tender and until the liquids are absorbed.
4. Mix the rice with the raisins, and pour the broth from the roasted lamb over it. If necessary, let it simmer for a while longer to absorb the liquids.
5. Sauté the kataifi noodles with the tablespoon of oil, until it browns and it is crunchy and add it to the rice.
6. Cut the lamb into portions and serve with the rice.

CHICKEN OR DUCK WITH OKRA

kotopoulo i papaki me bamies

Serves: 4-6

Preparation time: 30'   Cooking time: 60'   Degree of difficulty: △❍△   Nutritional value: △❍△

Taste: △❍△   Calories: 521

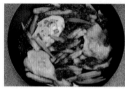

1 chicken or 1 duck 1 – 1½ kg.
(2.2 – 3.3 lb.) cut in pieces
1 kg. (2.2 lb.) okra
1 chopped onion
2 cups cubed tomatoes
2 sliced tomatoes
1 s.s. tomato paste diluted
in ½ cup hot water
6 s.s. chopped parsley
4 s.s. olive oil
salt, pepper and ½ t.s. sugar
For the marinade:
½ cup olive oil
2 cups white wine
3 s.s. vinegar / 2 bay leaves
1 s.s. granulated pepper

Preparation

1. If you use duck for this dish, rub the pieces of the duck with salt and pepper and marinade them for 1 day.

2. Sauté the bird pieces with the oil and when they brown add the onion and sauté until it also browns.

3. Add the cubes, the tomato paste, the salt, pepper and sugar and simmer for approximately 40', or until tender.

4. Cut off the top of the okra, where the stem is. Salt them, sprinkle them with a little vinegar, place them in a pan and place them in the sun for approximately 1 hour to dry, so that the sticky liquid in their interior dries. Wash the okra and place in a strainer. Add the okra to the stew and cook for approximately 20', so they won't mash.

5. Place the okra and the bird pieces in a heat resistant pan, distribute the tomato slices on top and sprinkle with the parsley.

6. Roast at 180° C for approximately 10', until the okra slightly scorches.

SWEETS

glika

RAISIN PIE
stafidopita

Serves: 12

Preparation time: 30'   Cooking time: 1 hour   Degree of difficulty: △❍△

Nutritional value: △△❍   Calories: 279

Preparation

500 gr. (1.1 lb.) hard flour
500 gr. (1.8 oz.) fresh or 1½ s.s. dry yeast
1½ cups lukewarm water
3 s.s. sugar
1 cup raisins
2 t.s. cinnamon
½ t.s. grated cloves
3 s.s. olive oil
½ t.s. salt
a little milk and sesame for garnishing

1. Mix the yeast with ½ cup water and 2-3 s.s. flour and place in a warm place to allow it to rise.

2. Sift the flour into a bowl, make a hole in the middle and add the yeast mixture and the remaining ingredients.

3. Knead the flour little-by-little until a soft, elastic dough is formed that can be easily moulded. Add a little more flour if needed.

4. Cover the dough and place it in a hot place for 2-3 hours, so it may rise and increase in volume to double its size.

5. Knead it again and then place in a pan. Cover again and allow it to rise.

6. Brush a little milk on the surface, sprinkle the sesame seeds on and bake at 200° C for 25'-30' until the raisin pie turns a golden brown.

CARROT CAKE
carrot cake

Serves: 14-16

Preparation time: 30'   Cooking time: 1 hour   Degree of difficulty: ❍△△

Nutritional value: △△❍   Calories: 288

Preparation

2½ cups self-raising flour
1½ cups sugar
4 eggs
1 cup olive oil
1 cup strained yoghurt
1 cup grated carrot
1 cup blanched and grated almonds
1 t.s. almond or vanilla extract

1. Beat the oil and sugar until it whitens.

2. Add the egg yolks one by one and continue to beat.

3. Add the yoghurt, flour and almond extract and continue to beat until it becomes a uniform puree. Add the carrots and almonds and mix well.

4. Beat the egg white meringue with a little salt and add to the cake mixture, mixing softly so that the meringue will not "drop".

5. Oil a mould, add the sifted flour followed by the mixture. Bake at 175° C for about 60'.

HONEY MACAROONS FILLED WITH WALNUTS
melomakarona gemista me karidia

Serves: 40-50 pieces
Preparation time: 30'   Cooking time: 30'   Degree of difficulty: △❍△
Nutritional value: △△❍   Calories: 306

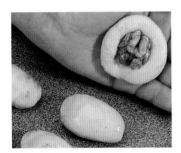

Preparation

For the dough:
1½ cups olive oil / ½ cup sugar
3/4 cup orange juice
1 s.s. orange rind
1 coffee cup cognac
1 packet baking powder
2 t.s. cinnamon / 6 cups flour
2 cups walnuts cut in half
For the syrup: 2 cups honey
2 cups sugar / 2 cups water
the rind of 1 lemon
2 cinnamon sticks
1 t.s. clove spikes
For garnishing:
cups coarsely grounded walnuts
cinnamon for sprinkling

1. Beat the oil and sugar until it whitens and add the juice, the rind of the orange and the cognac, and mix.

2. Sift the flour, baking powder and cinnamon into a bowl, make a hole in the middle and add the oil mixture.

3. Lightly knead the flour a little at a time. Add a little more flour if needed.

4. Take a piece of dough (about the size of a walnut), open it in the palm of your hand, place in it half a walnut and close it. Knead it until it becomes oval-shaped.

5. Place the macaroons in a row in the pan and flatten them a little with a fork or other kitchen utensil, so that they can be decorated. Bake at 180°C for about 30' until they brown.

6. Prepare the syrup by boiling the ingredients for 5'. Remove the macaroons from the oven, place them upside down in a clean pan or other container and pour the syrup over them. When the syrup has been absorbed, turn them again onto their other side.

7. When the macaroons have cooled down completely and have absorbed all the syrup, place them in a platter and sprinkle on walnuts and cinnamon.

LENTEN FRUIT TART
nistisimi tarta me frouta

Serves: 10-12

Preparation time: 15'   Cooking time: 30'   Degree of difficulty: ❍△△
Nutritional value: △△❍   Calories:

Preparation

For the dough:
1 cup flour
½ cup grated walnuts
3/4 t.s. baking powder
2 s.s. sugar
1/4 cup water
1 t.s. cinnamon
½ t.s. grated cloves
1/3 cup olive oil
For the filling:
½ cup jam
1 cup dried or glacé fruit
½ cup raisins
½ cup walnuts

1. Mix the flour with the oil and rub it to make it crumbly. Add the walnuts, baking powder, sugar and water and shape the dough into a ball. This dough does not need much kneading. Allow it to harden in the fridge for about 30'.

2. Roll out the dough onto a floured surface into the form of a round sheet, sized a little larger than the tart mould that it will be baked in, and place it into the mould.

3. Put some beans into the tart to prevent it from rising when baked, and bake it at 220°C for 20'. Lower the heat and bake at 190°C for another 8'.

4. Allow the tart to cool and spread on the jam. Sprinkle on the dried fruit and the walnuts.

CRULLERS
diples

Serves: 20

Preparation time: 60'   Cooking time: 10'   Degree of difficulty: △❍△
Nutritional value: △△❍   Calories: 320

Preparation

For the dough:
½ kg. (1.1 lb.) flour
½ t.s. soda / 3 eggs
the juice and rind
of 1 orange
1 coffee cup cognac
2 s.s. olive oil + enough oil
for frying
For the syrup: 1 cup honey
1 cup sugar / 1 cup water
lemon rind / 1-2 cinnamon sticks
For garnishing:
cup coarsely grounded walnuts
cinnamon

1. Sift the flour into a bowl, make a hole in the middle and add the soda, the orange juice and rinds, the softly beaten eggs the olive oil and the cognac.
2. Knead the flour little-by-little, until a dough is formed that can be moulded, without it sticking to the hands. Add a little more flour if needed.
3. Roll the dough into a thin sheet and cut long, narrow strips or some other shape.
4. Fry the crullers in hot oil and then place them on absorption paper to strain off the oil.
5. Prepare the syrup by boiling all the ingredients together for about 25'.
6. Place the crullers into the hot syrup, a few at a time, remove and place them on a platter with a skimmer. Sprinkle them with cinnamon and walnuts.

SEMOLINA CHALVA
chalvas simigdalenios

Serves: 16
Preparation time: 10'   Cooking time: 20'   Degree of difficulty: ❍△△
Nutritional value: △△❍   Calories: 345

Preparation

1 cup olive oil
2 cups coarse semolina
3 cups sugar
4 cups water
½ cup coarsely grounded
blanched almonds
½ cup sesame
the rind of 1 lemon
1 t.s. clove spikes
1 cinnamon stick
cinnamon for sprinkling

1. Boil the water with the sugar, the lemon rinds, the cinnamon stick and cloves for 5', then remove the aromatic spices.
2. Put the oil into a deep pot and warm. Add the semolina. Stir continuously on a medium fire, allowing the semolina to sauté. Add the almonds and the sesame and stir, together with the semolina, and sauté until they brown.
3. Remove the pot from the fire and carefully pour in the hot syrup. Again place the pot on the fire and boil the semolina on a low fire, stirring continuously, until it rises and all the syrup has been absorbed.
4. Place the chalva in a mould or individual cups and sprinkle with cinnamon. The chalva can be served hot or cold.

Note: This recipe is the traditional one for chalva (semolina) and housewives remember it as the 1, 2, 3, 4; i.e. 1 cup olive oil, 2 cups semolina, 3 cups sugar, 4 cups water. You can add less sugar if the chalva is too sweet for you.

CINNAMON COOKIES
koulourakia me kanela

Serves: 20
Preparation time: 50'   Cooking time: 15'   Degree of difficulty: ❍△△
Nutritional value: △△❍   Calories: 200

Preparation

500 gmgr. (1.1 lb.) flour
1 t.s. soda
1 t.s. baking powder
3/4 cup sugar
1 cup olive oil
2 s.s. cognac
7-8 s.s. water
3 t.s. cinnamon

1. Sift the flour into a bowl, make a hole in the middle and add all the remaining ingredients.
2. Knead the flour little-by-little, until the dough is hard enough to be moulded. Add a little more flour if needed.
3. Mould the dough into long, narrow cylinders and shape into various figures. Bake at 180° C for about 15'.

FRIED KNOTS
fiongakia tiganita

Serves: 10-12
Preparation time: 50'   Cooking time: 10'   Degree of difficulty: △◐△
Nutritional value: △△◐   Calories: 328

Preparation

250 gr. (8.8 oz.) flour
60 gr. (2.1 oz.) butter
2 s.s. sugar
1 t.s. vanilla
1 s.s. cognac
5 egg yolks
4 egg whites
olive oil for frying
icing sugar for garnishing

1. Beat the butter and sugar until it whitens and slowly add the yolks one by one, while continuing to beat the mixture. Add the vanilla and the cognac.
2. Beat the egg white meringue with a little salt and add to the butter mixture, mixing softly.
3. Sift the flour, make a hole in the middle and add the butter mixture.
4. Knead the flour little-by-little, until a dough is formed hard enough so that it can be easily moulded. Add a little more flour if needed.
5. Roll the dough into a thin sheet and cut strips about 15 cm long and 2 cm wide. Tie the strips into little knots.
6. Fry the little knots in hot oil and then place them on kitchen absorbent paper towels to strain off the oil.
7. Prepare the syrup by boiling all the ingredients together for about 25'.
8. Place the little knots on a platter and sprinkle them with icing sugar.

NUTMEG PIE
moshokaridopita

Serves: 20
Preparation time: 30'   Cooking time: 1 hour   Degree of difficulty: ◐△△
Nutritional value: △△◐   Calories: 301

Preparation

½ kg. (1,.1 lb.)
self-raising flour
1 cup olive oil / 1 ½ cups sugar
1 cup milk / 6 eggs
1 coffee cup cognac
1 cup walnuts
1 cup raisins
1 cup mixed dry fruit
1 t.s. each grated nutmeg
andf cinnamon

1. Beat the oil and sugar in a mixer until it whitens.
2. Put in the egg yolks one by one and continue beating.
3. Add the milk, cognac, flour and spices and beat the mixture until it becomes a uniform puree.
4. Beat the egg yolk meringue with very little salt and add the cake mixture, mixing softly so that the meringue will not "collapse".
5. Coat a pan with oil, sprinkle some flour and pour in the mixture. Bake in the oven at 175°C for about 1 hour.

SMALL APPLE PIES
milopitakia

Serves: 14-16

Preparation time: 40'   Cooking time: 30'   Degree of difficulty: △◐△

Nutritional value: △△◐   Calories: 322

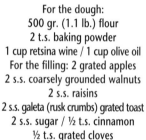

For the dough:
500 gr. (1.1 lb.) flour
2 t.s. baking powder
1 cup retsina wine / 1 cup olive oil
For the filling: 2 grated apples
2 s.s. coarsely grounded walnuts
2 s.s. raisins
2 s.s. galeta (rusk crumbs) grated toast
2 s.s. sugar / ½ t.s. cinnamon
½ t.s. grated cloves
icing sugar and cinnamon
for garnishing

Preparation

1. Sift the flour into a bowl, make a hole in the middle and add the baking powder, olive oil and retsina.

2. Knead the flour little-by-little, until a dough is formed that can be moulded, without it sticking to the hands. Add a little more flour if needed.

3. Mix all the ingredients for the filling.

4. Roll out the dough into thin pastry sheets about 3 mm thick and cut into disk shapes with a glass or a coup-pat.

5. Put a spoonful of filling onto each dough disk, wet the edges with a little water and fold in half to form half-moon shapes. Press the edges well to stick together, thus keeping the filling inside.

6. Bake the small apple pies at 200° C for 30' until they brown. Place in a platter and sprinkle with cinnamon and icing sugar.

ST. FANOURIOS PIE
fanouropita

Serves: 20
Preparation time: 30' Cooking time: 1 hour Degree of difficulty: ❍△△
Nutritional value: △△❍ Calories: 318

Preparation

500 gr. (1.1 lb.)
self-raising flour
1½ cups sugar
1 cup orange juice
and rinds
½ cup water
2/3 cup olive oil
1 cup coarsely grounded
walnuts
1 cup raisins
2 t.s. cinnamon
1 t.s. grated cloves

1. Beat the oil and sugar in a mixer until it whitens.
2. Add the orange juice and rinds, water, flour and spices and beat until the mixture becomes a uniform puree.
3. Add the raisins and walnuts and mix with a spoon.
4. Oil a baking pan, sprinkle with flour and pour in the mixture.
Bake at 175°C for about 1 hour.

Note: This St. Fanourios Pie is a traditional sweet. On 27th August, the festival of St. Fanourios, the housewives prepares the pies and take them to the church to be blessed by the priest. It is said that the saint reveals their "fortunes" to the young girls, and whatever a person desires, as well as that which each person desires, he asks the saint to reveal it to him and he in turn "promises" the saint a pie. The St. Fanourios Pie must be made with 7 or 9 ingredients and divided among as many people as possible.

NUT PIES FROM SIFNOS
skaltsounakia sifneika

Serves: 14-16
Preparation time: 40' Cooking time: 30' Degree of difficulty: △❍△
Nutritional value: △△❍ Calories: 258

Preparation

For the dough:
3 cups flour / 1 s.s. sugar
1 t.s. baking powder
2/3 cup water
the rind of 1 orange
1/3 cup olive oil
1 t.s. cinnamon
For the filling:
1 cup coarsely grounded walnuts
1 cup coarsely grounded
blanched almonds
½ cup kontita
1 t.s. grated cloves
the rind of 1 orange
½ cup honey
icing sugar for garnishing

1. Sift the flour into a bowl, make a hole in the middle and add the remaining ingredients for the dough.
2. Knead the flour little-by-little until a dough is formed that can be moulded, without it sticking to the hands. Add a little more flour if needed.
3. Mix all the ingredients for the filling, adding a little more honey to blend all the ingredients.
4. Roll out the dough into a thin sheet about 3 mm thick and cut into disk shapes with a glass or a coup-pat.
5. Put a spoonful of filling onto each dough disk, wet the edges with a little water and fold in half to form half-moon shapes. Press the edges well to stick together, thus keeping the filling inside.
6. Bake the nut pies at 175°C for 30' until they brown.
7. Sprinkle with rosewater, icing sugar and a little cinnamon.

LADY FINGERS
Rolled Fingers with Almonds from the Cypriat Cuisine
daktyla kirion

Serves: 6-8
Preparation time: 45' Cooking time: 15' Degree of difficulty: △❍△
Nutritional value: △△❍ Calories: 659

Preparation

For the dough:
2 cups flour / 1 s.s. margarine
3 s.s. olive oil / 1 t.s. salt
For the filling:
1 cup blanched
and grounded almonds
2 s.s. sugar / 1 t.s. cinnamon
2 s.s. anthotiro (cream cheese)
For the syrup:
2 cups sugar / 2 cups water
2 s.s. lemon juice / 2-3 cloves
1 cinnamon stick
some olive oil for frying

1. Mix the flour with the salt, margarine and oil and rub it to form crumbs. Add some lukewarm water and knead the dough well until it becomes soft and pliable. Allow the dough to "sit" for about 30'.
2. Mix together all the ingredients for the filling together in a bowl.
3. Prepare the syrup by boiling all the ingredients for 5'.
4. Roll out the dough into a thin sheet about 2 mm thick and cut into square pieces each about 8 x 8 cm.
5. Put 1 t.s. filling onto each square piece of dough, wet the edges with a little water so they will stick together and fold them into the shape of a "finger". Press the edges well to stick together, thus keeping the filling inside.
6. Fry the "fingers" in hot oil, remove with a skimmer and dip into the lukewarm syrup.
7. Remove them from the syrup with a skimmer and place onto a platter.

HONEY PUFFS
loukoumades

Serves: 10-12
Preparation time: 60' Cooking time: 10' Degree of difficulty: ❍△△
Nutritional value: △△❍ Calories: 351

For the dough: 1 3/4 cups flour
1 s.s. granulated dry yeast
½ cup milk / ½ cup water
1 s.s. sugar
2 s.s. olive oil + enough oil
for frying / a little salt
For the syrup: 1 cup honey
1 cup sugar / 1 cup water
lemon rinds
1-2 cinnamon sticks
For garnishing: Coarsely
grounded walnuts and cinnamon

Preparation

1. Put the yeast into water (it should be lukewarm) and dissolve it. Put all the ingredients for the filling into a bowl, add the the yeast, and beat them all together until it becomes a uniform smooth puree.
2. Cover the bowl and allow to sit in a warm place so that the dough can rise.
3. Fry spoonfuls of dough in hot oil, Remove the honey puffs from the oil and place on kitchen absorption paper towels to drain off the oil.
4. Place the honey puffs on a platter, pour syrup on them and sprinkle them with cinnamon and walnuts.
5. The honey puffs are always served hot immediately after they are fried.

CRETAN TURBAN PIES
sarikopites kritikes

Serves: 20-22 pieces
Preparation time: 50' Cooking time: 10' Degree of difficulty: △△◐
Nutritional value: △△◐ Calories: 360

Preparation

For the dough:
500 gr. (1.1 lb.) flour
3 s.s. olive oil
2 s.s. tsikoudia (raki)
or lemon juice
1 cup water / a little salt
For the filling:
700 gr. (1 lb., 8 oz.) anthotiro
(cream cheese) or xynomyzithra
(sour skim-milk cheese)
½ cup sugar
1 t.s. cinnamon
½ t.s. nutmeg
some olive oil for frying
honey and cinnamon for serving

1. Sift the flour into a bowl, make a hole in the middle and add the olive oil, tsikoudia and salt.
2. Add a little water and taking a little flour at a time, knead it slowly, adding enough water so that a dough is formed that is not too hard and can be shaped, without it sticking to the hands.
3. Mix together all the ingredients for the filling.
4. Roll out the dough into a thin sheet about 3 mm thick and cut into strips about 20 cm long and 7 cm wide.
5. Put a spoonful of filling onto each dough strip, spreading it along the length of the dough. Wet the edges with a little water and wrap the dough strip into a small cylinder, thus forming a long, slender cylinder. Press the edges well to stick together, thus keeping the filling inside.
6. Wrap the dough strips into the form of a snail or a turban and fry in hot oil until they brown. Place the sarikopites onto a platter, douse with honey or a syrup similar to that described in the honey puff (loukoumades) recipe and sprinkle with cinnamon.
7. Sprinkle with rosewater, icing sugar and a little cinnamon.

BIBLIOGRAPHY

Colette Estin, Helen Laporte, Το Βιβλίο της Μυθολογίας, Gallimard, 1987

Ferrara LA, Raimondi AS, d'Episcopo L, Guida L, Dello Russo A, Marotta T. Olive Oil and Reduced Need for Antihypertensive Medications. Arch Intern Med. 2000 Mar 27

Gavalas Elaine. The World's Healthiest Diets. Oldways, Issue Nov., 2000

Giugliano D. Dietary Antioxidants for Cardiovascular Prevention. Nutr Metab Cardiovasc Dis. 2000 Feb;10

Keys A. Seven countries: A multivariate analysis of death and coronary health disease. Cambridge MA/London: Harvard University Press, 1980

Kush LH, Lenart EB, Willet WC. Health Implications of Mediterranean Diets in Light of Contemporary Knowledge. Part 2. Meat, wine, fats and oil. Am J Clin Nutr 1995

Manuel Vazquez Montalban, Ανήθικες Συνταγές, Δελφίνι, Αθήνα, 1995

P. Decharme, Ελληνική Μυθολογία, Φάρος, Αθήνα, 1960

S Renaud, M de Lorgeril, J Delaye, J Guidollet, F Jacquard, N Mamelle, JL Martin, I Monjaud, P Salen and P Toubol. Cretan Mediterranean Diet for Prevention of Coronary Heart Disease. American Journal of Clinical Nutrition, Vol 61

The Royal Hortricultural Society Plants and Flowers Encyclopedia. Dorling Kindersley, London, 1989

The Wellness Encyclopedia of Nutrition, University of California at Berkeley, Rebus, New York, 1992

Trichopoulou A., Katsoyanni K. and Gnardellis Ch., The Traditional Greek Diet.

European Journal of ClinicalNutrition 47, Suppl. I, Macmillan Press Ltd 1993) Wilson Cristine S. Mediterranean Diets: Once and Future Oldways, Issue Nov., 1998.

World Cancer Research Fund/American Institute for Cancer Research. Food, Nutrition and the Prevention of Cancer: A Global Perspective. Washington: American Institutes for Cancer Research, 1997.

Ανδρέας Στάλκος, Επικίνδυνες Μαγειρικές, Άγρα, Αθήνα, 1997

Μαυρομάτου-Χατζηκωντή Κλαίρη. Γεραγώτικοι Αντικατοπτρισμοί, Φωτογραφικό και Λαογραφικό Οδοιπορικό στη Γέρα της Λέσβου. Δήμος Γέρας, 2001
Με τη Νοστιμιά του Ελαιόλαδου. Έκδοση στα πλαίσια του Προγράμματος για την Κατανάλωση του Ελαιόλαδου. Ε.Ο.Κ. 1988-1989

Electronic addresses for further information on olive oil:
http: //www.nut.uoa.gr/
European Olive Oil Medical Information Library: http://europa.eu.int/comm/
American Dietetic Association (ADA): http://www.eatright.org/
American Journal of Clinical Nutrition: secretar@ascn.faseb.org
American Society for Clinical Nutrition: http://www.faseb.org/asns
American Society for Nutritional Sciences: http://www.faseb.org/ascn/
International Institute for Olive Oil: http://www.internationaloliveoil.org/
International Olive Oil Council: http:/www.internationaloliveoil.org/
Mayo Clinic Health Oasis: http://www.mayohealth.org/
Oldways: http://www.oldwayspt.org
http://my.webmd:com/http:/
http://www.dotpharmacy.com/upmed.html
http://heartinfo/org/nutrition/medit3398.htm

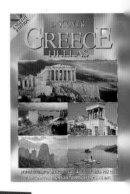

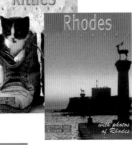